journeyed to change the rules and achieved tremendous success. I found the book to be informative, inspiring, and uplifting. Ralph Groce has the potential to help change a system that needs innovative ideas. I truly enjoyed this read.
> *Charly Palmer | Owner, Charly Palmer Fine Art*

Marvelous thought provoking read that will challenge your thinking, engage your mind with possibilities and motivate you to become part of the coalition of change making the world a better place.
> **Cynthia Cohen | Founder and Chief Strategist, IMPACT 2040**

WE HAVE NOTHING TO LOSE

A DARK OPTIMIST'S CALL TO ACTION

BY RALPH H. GROCE III

Copyright © 2024 Ralph H. Groce III
Published in the United States by Leaders Press.
www.leaderspress.com

All rights reserved. No part of this book may be reproduced or transmitted in any form or by any means, electronic or mechanical, including photocopying, recording, or by any information storage and retrieval system, except by a reviewer who may quote brief passages in a review to be printed in a magazine or newspaper. The contents of this book may not be used to train large language models or other artificial intelligence products without written permission
from the copyright holder.

ISBN **978-1-63735-325-7** (pbk)
ISBN **978-1-63735-326-4** (hcv)
ISBN **978-1-63735-324-0** (ebook)

Library of Congress Control Number: **2024913127**

Foreword

Ralph Groce didn't need to write *We Have Nothing to Lose: A Dark Optimist's Call to Action*. His professional and career successes and accomplishments speak for themselves. Having worked at the most prestigious financial and technology institutions on Wall Street and around the world, an argument could certainly be made that he deserves a peaceful, easy transition into his next chapter, whatever that may entail.

But if you know Ralph like I do, then you know it simply isn't in his DNA to take the easy path, even when he has earned it. Ralph wrote this book to challenge you and me to think differently, to embrace that which we share, and to acknowledge and even celebrate the differences that seemingly divide us. Indeed, what you have in your hands is more than a book; it's a call to action for engaged citizens who see our nation splintering in ways that truly should concern everyone. It's bold and audacious, because that is precisely what is needed to repair the divide in our country and restore a sense of community and civic mindedness that we have most certainly lost as a nation.

In his relatable and accessible writing style, Ralph illustrates his major points with personal and professional examples that help anchor and reinforce his major points such as the key elements of his agenda for positive change, while also reminding us of the simple yet incredibly powerful acts of conversing and listening with empathy. Starting with a very big-picture and strategic overview of the problem that we currently face, Ralph moves the reader through understanding and defining the role of the Presidency and a Constitutional Republic as we face the enormous challenges of immigration, gun violence and climate change. He then describes both the human factors and dynamics of coalitions, coupled with the role of technology, that must work in concert together to bring about positive, sustainable change.

What I particularly like about this book is that the ray of hope that springs forth from an admittedly "dark optimist." Research in resiliency and high performance, including the well-known "Stockdale Paradox" made famous in Jim Collins management classic *Good to Great*, demonstrates that transformation can only occur when we can simultaneously stare down reality with cool objectivity, while also holding out a grounded and gritty hope – dark optimism if you will – that a brighter future is ahead. Ralph doesn't pull any punches, and he doesn't offer an easy path forward because one doesn't exist. However, he offers a grounded hope in a thoughtful and comprehensive roadmap that we must follow collectively if we are to actualize a better future for this nation and the generations that will follow us.

William L. Sparks, Ph.D.
Author, *Actualized Teamwork: Unlocking the Culture Code for Optimal Performance*
http://www.DrWillSparks.com

Table of Contents

Foreword vii

About the Author xiii

Introduction xv

Chapter 1 1
    What the World Needs Now 1
    The Power of Diversity 2
    Our Place in the Universe 4
    Challenges Strengthen Us 6
    Working Toward a Solution 8

Chapter 2 11
    Defining the Presidency 11
    Reinventing the Wheel 13
    Challenges with Our Constitutional Republic 15
    It's Not About Me 17

Chapter 3 21
    The Gap Between Promises and Delivery 21
    The Challenges 22
    Divisive Technology 23
    Being Accountable 25
    What Did *You* Do? 27
    Technology for Good 28

Chapter 4 31
    The Power of Unity 31
    A Shared Model of Success 31
    Our Divisions Are Deepening 34
    Issues to Address 35
    Dark Optimism 37
    Moments of Unity 40
    The Challenge Ahead 41
    Getting There 44

Chapter 5 47
Defining the Agenda for Change 47
Immigration 48
Gun Violence: An Unacceptable Normalcy 49
Climate Change 51
Returns on Investment 51
Storytelling Tools 53
Leaving a Roadmap 55
The Role of Technology 56

Chapter 6 61
The First Task as President 61
Building a Team 61
Areas of Focus 62
Leveraging Technology 63
Listening to the People 63
Building Unity 64
The Point Guard President 66
Universal Truths 67

Chapter 7 71
Facilitating a Coalition of the Willing 71
Creating the Vision 72
Many Voices, One Chorus 74
Sudden, Drastic Change 76
Everyone Has Good Intentions 77
The Velocity of Change 79
Transformational Experience Counts 82
Persuasion vs. Coercion 83

Chapter 8 85
The Power of Conversations 85
Harnessing the Superpower of Communications 89
Effective Communication and the Ethical Dilemma of Social Media 93
The Stories We Remember 94
The Art of Turning 'Impossible' Into 'Achievable' 96

Chapter 9 99
    Thriving Amidst Flux 99
    Championing Transformation: The Journey to Excellence 102
    Queue the Black Swans 104
    Running for the Bus 108
    It Is Our Legacy 109

Chapter 10 113
    A Coalition of the Willing 113
    Embracing Empathy 116

Chapter 11 121
    Technology and Leadership 121
    Fostering Technological Progress: The Endless Frontier Act 123
    Harnessing AI for Good 125
    The World Is Changing 128

Afterword 133

About the Author

Ralph H. Groce III is an accomplished entrepreneur, visionary thinker, and dedicated advocate for change. He has a rich tapestry of experiences in entrepreneurship, technology, finance, and philanthropy. He brings a unique perspective to the world of literature.

Ralph's journey has been one of self-determination, accountability, and entrepreneurial spirit. His parents, whom he refers to as "tiger parents on steroids," instilled in him a commitment to shape a better future. From his early dreams of becoming president of the United States to his illustrious career as an entrepreneur, Ralph's path has been marked by innovation, determination, and a relentless pursuit of excellence.

As a seasoned entrepreneur, Ralph has founded and successfully managed multiple businesses. He holds five patents, and his ventures have been at the forefront of innovation, contributing to economic growth and creating opportunities.

Ralph graduated from Boston University's Questrom School of Business and earned a Master of Urban Affairs degree from its Metropolitan College. Ralph also has an MBA from the McColl School of Business at Queens University in Charlotte, North Carolina, and an honorary doctorate from Johnson C. Smith University, also based in Charlotte.

Ralph has been a senior executive with several global financial services companies and has previously worked at Bankers Trust, Deutsche Bank, JPMorgan Chase, MetLife, Wachovia, Everest Re, BNY, and Wells Fargo. He has served on the boards of Fresh Youth Initiatives in New York City and the Socrates Academy in Charlotte. He has also served as a mentor for the Covenant House Rites of Passage program in New York City, and a mentor and professional advisor to the GENTS program at Vance High School in Charlotte.

Ralph currently serves on the Board of Trustees at Johnson C. Smith University and on the Boston University Advisory Board and is chairman of the Boston University Metropolitan College Advisory Board.

Ralph was raised in Pittsburgh, a city known for its resilience and innovation. Ralph's diverse passions include music, art, literature, technology, sports, and travel. His interests reflect his belief that a well-rounded life fosters creativity and personal growth.

Philanthropy holds a special place in Ralph's heart. His deep commitment to giving back to the community and making a positive impact on the lives of others is a driving force in his entrepreneurial journey.

We Have Nothing to Lose: A Dark Optimist's Call to Action is an embodiment of his vision for a brighter future, and his life's work is a testament to his commitment to leadership, and positive change.

Introduction

I was born and raised in Pittsburgh, but I knew from an early age that the city didn't suit me. It felt like a set of clothes that just did not fit properly. The garment felt too tight, too itchy. The stitching was loose, and I was in a perpetual state of discomfort. Ours was a predominantly African American neighborhood, one of the poorest and, particularly in recent years, one of the most crime ridden.

Though Pittsburgh did not feel right to me, it has twice been voted one of the most livable cities in the country and in the world. So, from this point of view, Pittsburgh is the tale of two cities—the one that I fled and the one that draws newcomers to its affordable housing, riverfront development, quality healthcare, and cultural and recreational opportunities. That dichotomy and my lingering discomfort with the city have prompted me to become actively involved in philanthropic efforts to make Pittsburgh even better, for everyone, than it already is.

Still, when I was young, getting out of Pittsburgh was paramount. I needed to escape. I remember at the age of nine asking my mother, "Could I have my own apartment?" That didn't happen, of course, but I immediately fled the city when I completed high school. I graduated on a Friday evening and was on the first bus out of Pittsburgh at eight o'clock the following morning. I escaped to Virginia Beach, where I spent the summer living and working with my uncle before starting my freshman year at Boston University.

When did this idea of running for president arise? Kindergarten. I recall being in class as the teacher went around and asked everyone, "What do you want to be when you grow up?" For some reason, and I could not tell you why, I said "I want to be president of the United States." I had aspirations, but my teacher thought I had something else in mind. She called my mother to let her know I was being disruptive in class. These delusional utterances!

As I think back on that period of my life, I realize how far we've come. I wasn't trying to call attention to myself or make myself a nuisance or trigger a hail of laughter from my classmates. Instead, my declaration was a testament to what I'll call my foresight and vision.

But it is also a testament to how I have always seemed to live on the fringes.

I was bused to predominately White schools outside of my community, which contributed mightily to feeling as though I didn't fit in anywhere. I didn't know many people in my neighborhood because we were not allowed to hang out with them. My days consisted solely of school and church. As I grew older and began playing basketball, all I ever did was go to the gym, church, and school.

When I reached seventh grade, Pittsburgh tested every seventh grader in the city, and the top students were put into two magnet schools with special classes, segregated from the rest of the student population. I was one of only two African Americans selected for these advanced schools. Everywhere I went, I felt as though I was just one in a group of one, and in many ways that feeling persists to this day.

I chose to attend Boston University. That was an intentional choice. I'll talk about the concept of intentionality and the power of choice throughout this book—it is one of the principles and part of the philosophy that guides my life—and going to BU was an embodiment of that attitude. Frankly, I could have gone to any one of a number of top-flight schools. I received a lot of literature from schools across the country professing interest in having me attend.

Given my aforementioned feelings about Pittsburgh, it wasn't difficult for me to determine that no school in the city of Pittsburgh was far enough away. (That eliminated a number of great schools!) No school in the state of Pennsylvania was far enough away either. In fact, no school in any state bordering Pennsylvania was far enough away. I wanted to be far enough away that returning to Pittsburgh would be difficult, even if I wanted to do so.

We couldn't afford for me to visit any campuses, so I was left leafing through literature to find things of interest, such as people who looked like me. In many cases, I didn't see very many who did.

A math professor for one of my advanced courses heard that Boston University was interested in me, and he strongly encouraged me to go there. "You have to go to Boston," he said. "Any school in Boston. Boston is the academic mecca of the country, possibly the world." BU was one of the few schools offering me opportunities outside of engineering, so I selected Boston.

Boston was a revelation. Going to school there was a transformative experience. And it continues to be! Part of the reason I remain so committed to and involved with Boston University is because I want to ensure that others who come from a background like mine and look like me have access to the same type of experience I had at BU.

And it really was a transformation.

Boston presented me with an opportunity to reinvent myself. I could explore parts of myself that I couldn't in Pittsburgh because, where people know you—or think they know you—they often feel threatened if you speak, dress, or act in a manner that they don't expect or want from you. It becomes difficult to evolve when people put you in a box that is comfortable for them and object if you attempt to escape that box and evolve. Boston represented an opportunity to shed that box and start anew. I was able to evolve in Boston. It was an amazing awakening. The people that I met, the courses I took, the educators I became involved with, and the experiences I had were all part of an extraordinary transformative awakening.

Basketball played a significant role in that experience. I began playing serious basketball later in life than most kids, but I made dramatic improvements in high school. I didn't receive athletic scholarship offers from any Division I schools. Nevertheless, one of my criteria for choosing a college was that it had to have a Division I men's basketball program that I could try out for as a walk-on. Basketball was my and remains a passion of mine. I've always felt I wanted to be the biggest fish in the biggest pond. I want to compete against the best. I want to be surrounded by the best. I want to understand the standards and the mindset of the best. I want to be counted among the best. That's the way I was raised. And that's the mindset that I've always had.

Boston University offered me not only one of the best academic schools in the country but also a chance to play at the highest level.

It was a fantastic journey. I had the opportunity to play for Rick Pitino, a Hall of Fame coach and one of the best basketball minds in the world. He affected the way I thought and introduced me to new concepts. In many ways, Rick validated the concepts my father and mother had pointedly stressed to me in Pittsburgh. My father never met Rick Pitino, but the similarities between the two are absolutely amazing. I remember coming home from school and once in a while not having straight As or having not been ranked the best in the class. That resulted in intense punishment. I would insist that I'd done my best and my father would respond, "I'm not interested in your best. The only thing that matters is you *being* the best."

That standard has been the standard I have always measured myself against. And it can be challenging.

After completing my undergraduate degree, I continued on to grad school—I didn't feel ready to go into the real world—and that extra year was instrumental in helping me mature and figure out my next steps. In time, I decided New York City was where I needed to be. I had always been fascinated by New York. Over the course of my undergrad and grad tenure, I met a lot of people from New York who impressed me with their perspectives, their swagger, and their worldliness. New York came to represent that big pond with the big fish that I wanted to be in. I was particularly fascinated with Wall Street. (My father had also always been interested in Wall Street. He was an individual investor at a time when that was highly uncommon.) So, after grad school, I moved to New York looking for fame and fortune.

The plan was simple: move to New York, work on Wall Street, become a trader, make a billion dollars, run for mayor of New York, and then run for President of the United States.

The plan got a little twisted, but here I am, still working in New York and enjoying a career in technology and on Wall Street. It's been a thrilling ride. My career has not been a straight line to the top—I would describe it as more of a zigzag path—but my drive has been relentless. I awake every day with a sense of purpose and urgency. It is not in my nature to be patient—why can't we get things done now? I want to know—so I push, I work, I rage against the machine, and I get things done. I probably wear out my welcome sooner than most because I'm not content to merely pay my dues and wait. I can't afford to waste time idly waiting.

My energy and insistence have brought profound changes to some organizations, but they can also create a turbulent wake.

I believe in the power of intellect; I believe in the power of knowledge. One of my favorite comic book characters, Dr. Doom says, "Only through more and greater knowledge can I gain the power I seek." Education has always been important to me. Growing up, I actually looked forward to summer school! To this day, I find myself constantly consuming information and acquiring knowledge. I am curious about the world around me and why things are the way they are. I'm curious about how we can make them better. I'm curious about how I can make myself better. I'm curious how I can help others and help them be better.

Education is a big part of my philanthropic efforts because I believe more, and better knowledge will save the world. The more educated people we can get around the table, the more we enhance our opportunities to make better decisions.

My entrepreneurial work has been very important to me. My drive compels my entrepreneurial endeavors. I left Deutsche Bank because I believed I was ready to be a CEO. When I wasn't made CEO, I went out on my own and started a self-funded enterprise called GroceProfit. Our mission was to address income inequality and provide a way for people of color and women to invest in equity markets. My research indicated that African Americans don't invest in equity markets the way whites do. My efforts were centered on providing education, tools, and a call to action to help bridge the gap. We made great progress. We had a trading platform, licensed content, and a mechanism to clear and settle trades. Unfortunately, I was unable to raise the angel and venture capital to keep the company going.

However, I would not hesitate to do it again. There is a real need for this kind of service. It's also true that I learned a great deal through this effort. The challenges I faced and the growth I experienced had a profound and powerful impact on my life, so that years later, I started another company.

This new effort is an art gallery called Knowhere, which is a name somewhat inspired in part by my beloved Marvel comics. I created a vision and a mission around the business. We have a saying: K equals E squared. A mathematician would write it this way: $K = e^2$. What we mean by that is that Knowledge equals Enlightenment to the second power. As your knowledge grows, your enlightenment compounds at an exponential rate.

The goal of the gallery is to share knowledge and create enlightenment and to make people challenge their way of thinking, particularly their sense of themselves and their place in the world. We want them to challenge their conceptions of the world with the art we display. It's also an opportunity to do some of the things that I was trying to do with GroceProfit. Any diverse portfolio should include art, so we discuss with people who are buying art for the first time why this investment can help them build sustainable wealth. We have also invested in creating and leveraging artificial intelligence, VR, and AR in art. We're also exploring opportunities to look at blockchain and smart contracts associated with the art that we sell.

A lot of people don't think that I have an artistic side. However, I am an intricate blend of art and science—a kind of Spock-like figure who has a human and Vulcan side. I use logic and reason to manage the fury and ambition that fuel me.

Writing this book and running for president pulls all of these elements of my personality together. They satisfy the artistic part of my personality and allow me to talk about changing the lives of people from the perspective of how they live, what they do, and how they do it. It allows me to bring technology into something that a lot of people don't think can have a technological bent.

I presently hold multiple patents. I hear a lot of people talk about how innovative I am, but I don't think of myself that way. What I really am is impatient. I want what I want, and I want exactly what I want, right now. If I can't get it, I invent it.

Elon Musk works that way. What he has done with Tesla and with this Cybertruck—having to literally invent a new way of building something in order to create this thing that he introduced to the world several years ago—has been fascinating to watch. Musk is impatient. He wants to know, why can't we have reusable rockets? Why do we have to throw those things away? Why can't we create something that we can reuse? He asked that question and now—*voila*—he's doing it.

I have always operated in a similar manner. Moreover, I've never had a job for which I was qualified.

Typically, jobs come with a job description. Here's the person we're looking for. This person has done this. This person knows this. This person is an expert in that. I typically don't have any of those qualifications.

For example, I started my career as an assistant buyer in men's sportswear for Lord & Taylor. I was the assistant to the head buyer, an amazing woman who bought men's sports outfits from all over the world. My job was to put these garments on the floor and then accessorize them. But I am colorblind, and the head buyer learned that the second she examined my display of the clothing and its accessories. She went nuts.

Although that part of my career didn't last too long, I was actually good at it and quickly transitioned to the business part of the retail industry, which preceded my foray into financial services and the banking industry.

I was equally unqualified to work in banking, but that career has worked out well for me. One of my first jobs was to oversee a group that manually authenticated senders moving money from one account to another. Within four months, I had completely automated the process and displaced nearly all of the people working in that area. I did this in other areas, and at one point, I was asked by the regional head of operations at Deutsche Bank to take over our Y2K preparation and our transition to the euro. The problem was we were only fourteen months away from migrating to the euro and we had done nothing. We didn't even know what instruments we needed to convert to euros.

We're talking here about managing wholesale conversion of Deutsche North America to the euro. I'd never done anything on that scale. I had never managed a project that large or complex. Now, why would Deutsche put me in charge of something so vital? I wondered, so I asked the executive: why me?

"Because I believe you will figure it out," he said. "I've watched you and I've seen you go from knowing nothing, understanding nothing, to being an expert in whatever I have put in front of you. So, I'm confident you'll figure it out. And you are one of the few people who is unencumbered by what you don't know. That doesn't scare you. I also get the sense that you're not scared of the repercussions if you fail. I'll fire you."

"You're right," I said. "I will figure it out. And I'm not scared about being fired either."

Within fourteen months, I had not only nailed the conversion but was driving the conversion on a global scale for Deutsche Bank. I'd also navigated the Y2K issue.

This was just the first of many opportunities to complete projects for which I was not prepared. I remember interviewing at Wachovia for a job managing the corporate trust and retirement businesses.

"What do you know about the retirement business?" my prospective boss asked me.

"I don't know anything about it," I replied.

"What do you know about corporate trust?"

"Not much."

"Have you ever led a development team? You've ever led a team of engineers and developers?"

"No, haven't done that."

"So, why are we here? Why should I hire you? "

I talked to him about what I brought to the table. I talked about my leadership acumen. I recounted how many times I had gone from not knowing anything to being an expert and leader in whatever space I focused on. I talked about my ability to build high-performing teams. I talked about how I drive and create technology in a manner that accentuates and aligns with business objectives and creates extraordinary value by constructing solutions that consistently deliver sustainable and scalable competitive advantages. I was one of the best in the country at doing that. I fully understood my personal value proposition.

I got the job. I did the job. And I exceeded their expectations. I even exceeded expectations they didn't know they had.

I suspect that as we move forward with my presidential aspirations, that sort of ability is going to come in handy. The White House is another job for which I am probably not qualified, but there's no doubt in my mind that given the opportunity, I will transform this country and the world.

Read on and find out how I plan to do that.

Chapter 1

What the World Needs Now

A Canadian power company was faced with an intractable problem. Every winter, condensation would cause icicles to form on their power lines. Over time, the icicles would grow and get heavier until, at one point, they would snap the lines and cut power to hundreds of thousands of people.

This is Canada. It's cold. When it's frigid and thousands of homes and businesses lose power, the ramifications ripple across the icy landscape. Hospitals struggle. Commerce shuts down. Communication lines fall silent. People die.

So, the power company pulled together a group of experts to brainstorm some answers. The people at the table came from all walks of life—engineers, politicians, law enforcement, and meteorologists—and the only rule was this: No idea is a bad idea. The utility wanted a free flow of ideas, hoping that somewhere among that storm of thoughts, an answer would emerge.

The ideas soon started to flow. Some had been tried before and hadn't worked. Some were simply impractical or too expensive. After a time, the group seemed to be at an impasse. People grew quiet, frustrated. They sat back in their chairs and stared at the ceiling, quietly concentrating on finding a solution.

"Too bad we couldn't train a bunch of bears to patrol those power lines," one person said finally, trying to break the tense silence with humor. "Bears love icicles. They suck on them for water. If we could train them to shake the poles and dislodge those icicles, the problem would disappear."

A few people sighed, and some rolled their eyes. They must be failing if the ideas were this bad, some thought. But others sat up and leaned over the table, their eyes intent.

"Shake the poles," one said.

"Create some vibration. Knock the icicles loose," another said.

A hard, sharp silence fell as the entire room concentrated on that notion.

"What about ... *helicopters?*" a participant asked. "Could they fly along the power lines and use the vibration of the rotor blades to knock the ice free?"

Yes, they could. And they did. The company was soon employing a fleet of helicopters to regularly fly over the company's cross-country powerlines, scouting for ice problems, and then swooping down to use turbulence from their rotor blades to dislodge the ice and keep the power flowing. That winter, the number of power outages was a fraction of what it had been in the past.

I use that story whenever I lead a brainstorming session in my role as a technologist. To me, it demonstrates the power of ideas and how one idea can build on another and then another until you have a solution far better than any you could have imagined. Before you know it, you arrive at a place that's novel—as well as distinctive, workable, practical, and utterly doable.

The Power of Diversity

The story also demonstrates the power of diversity of thought. Our country is facing a great many challenges today, and some of them—including climate change, political divisiveness, gun violence, and the repression of minority voices—are truly daunting. They are so fearsome that many wonder if there can ever be a solution to them. Our country, however, also has an extraordinary amount of diversity that offers people from around the world the opportunity to come here and become part of something that gives them a chance to be their authentic selves and contribute their ideas.

Our country is a mosaic. Steve Jobs was an adopted immigrant. He changed the world. One of the founders of Google was an immigrant. Elon Musk, whether you like him or not, is having a huge impact on our world of transportation, space travel, and social media, and he's also an immigrant. The mosaic includes people of color, different ethnicities, different religious affiliations, and people of different genders. Throughout the history of this country, we have benefited from the extraordinary contributions of all of these groups, such as the three black women whose calculations helped our country win the Space Race. Apple used to run a commercial with the tagline "Think different," and that is what people in this country have done time and again to overcome what are seemingly intractable circumstances and situations.

So, I'm a big believer in the power of diversity and in our ability to solve huge problems. As a technologist, I've seen it happen. A bunch of people like me sitting around a table solving a problem might be interesting. Something good might come out of that brainstorming. However, if you start mixing that up, then, my God, the things that people come up with as a result of these different perspectives are unbelievable. It's literally jaw-dropping. Again, I've seen it. I've been part of it. It's life-affirming. It's life-changing.

I've been asked to help solve problems where, when we sat down, the prevailing sense was that there was no freaking way we would succeed. There's just no way that this can get done. And an hour later, five hours later, a day later, a weekend later, we walk away saying "Wow, what just happened?" And it was all a function of people bringing diverse ideas to the table.

There's another story involving servicemen fighting in Iraq after 9/11. They frequently found themselves walking into booby-trapped buildings and sustaining casualties when they encountered nearly invisible tripwires. It was a real problem, and you can imagine the stress these soldiers were under every day. But then one day, someone had an idea.

Supportive Americans were sending soldiers care packages, and for some reason, they started including Silly String along with cookies and other treats. Silly String. You press the button, and the canister sends a stream of ultra-lightweight material across the room. So, the soldiers on patrol in Iraqi cities began spraying the Silly String into rooms before they entered. As the lightweight blasts of Silly String settled, they would drape over the thin booby-trap wires, revealing them but not triggering them.

Again, it's that kind of innovation that happens at the nexus of diversity and inclusion.

Having been all around the world and seen incredible places and met fascinating people, what I come back to is that other places don't have all this diversity. But we have it. It's our secret weapon.

Look at what happens when we go to the Olympics. Why does the U.S. win so many medals? Other countries have great athletes and facilities. They have exceptional training methods. Some even use drugs to improve their athletes' performance. But no one brings the same diversity to the athletic field as the U.S. Half of our medals come from our female athletes. A great number come from people of color. Other countries don't have that (or don't allow it). And as a result, they don't have a shot against us because our diversity gives us strength.

Our Place in the Universe

I'm friends with a group of guys I've known for over twenty years, and we have an online chat room where we share our ideas and reflections on our lives and the world. Nothing formal. It's a virtual locker room of sorts. One of the questions that somebody recently posed was, "Are we alone in the universe?"

I was reminded of the Fermi paradox. The idea, articulated by Italian-American physicist Enrico Fermi, posits that there is a discrepancy between the scant evidence of advanced extraterrestrial life and the apparently high likelihood that such life exists. In 1950, as Fermi was having lunch with Edward Teller, Herbert York, and Emil Konopinski and discussing recent reports of unidentified flying objects, Fermi noted that since many of the sun-like stars are billions of years older than our sun, the Earth should already have been visited by extraterrestrial civilizations. But there is no convincing evidence that this has happened. It's a paradox. Recently, however, some researchers using mathematical models concluded that there is a high degree of probability that we are indeed alone.

As the conversation progressed, the commentary moved to the conclusion that if that's true, then our responsibility to this planet and life on Earth increases exponentially—astronomically, if you will. We need to conduct ourselves and treat one another in a way that respects not only the life that's here today but also the billions and billions of potential lives that will come after us.

This brings me back to all of the things that are happening right now. The Doomsday Clock is the closest it has ever been to twelve o'clock. Public officials are being indicted for serious crimes against our democracy. We have $82 trillion invested in venture capital, and less than 2 percent is going to businesses started by women and people of color. Not only are there biases in the physical world and a lack of diversity around the table, but those biases and lack of diversity are also becoming part of the virtual world created by artificial intelligence. AI, we need to remember, is relentless. It never slows down. It never takes a break. And despite all the benefits AI may add to our lives, the idea that we don't have a representative group of people around the table to ensure that these tools act responsibly and equitably is really, really scary. These things weigh heavily on my mind every day.

The world is burning. This country is burning. That's a challenge. But within that, we have an extraordinary opportunity for people to step forward, speak up, and take a position. I'm not talking about a position that declares that everyone who doesn't think like you is from hell but a position that says, "Let's figure out a path forward that works." Let's figure out a path forward that is inclusive, brings equity, and addresses climate change, equity, and social justice issues. Let's confront the threats to our democracy. Let's confront the inequities that we have. Let's confront the challenges we have and do so in a manner that solves these issues!

Challenges Strengthen Us

Not long ago, a 32-year-old former medal-winning U.S. Olympic sprinter died during childbirth. It was hard to believe that it could happen in our country, but when you look at the statistics, we learn that, among all Western nations, the United States is one of the most dangerous countries in the world to have a child. That's true irrespective of your race, but the statistics are even more dire when you start breaking that information down demographically. It's insane. No woman should have to face the prospect of dying during childbirth, an event of extraordinary joy. But it's true: despite all of the resources we have in this country, death during childbirth is a very realistic prospect for a significant number of women in this country.

That's unacceptable, but these conditions have persisted so long that they've become entrenched in our way of life. They've become something we accept and simply shrug off. And that's just not who we should be as a country. That is not who we should be as a people. That is not who we should be as a world.

I don't want to sound Pollyannaish. I'm not looking to create a utopia. I think challenges are good. Challenges make us strong. Iron needs fire. Diamonds need pressure. The best things in life come when we earn them, often through trial and error, failure and joy, and winning. Without that effort, we just don't get to the best of who we are. Our country has a special responsibility—to ourselves, to the citizens of this country, and to the world—to be an example of what the best can be. But we are not living up to that example today.

These challenges we face should not create the kind of turmoil that is persisting and pervading every facet of our lives in this country. When these challenges are left unchecked and unaddressed, we are not honoring the special privilege we have as living, sentient creatures in this universe. Are we alone in the universe? We seem to be, despite the vastness of the universe and the paradox inherent in that. Against the backdrop of an infinite universe, what we have is truly, truly precious, and we clearly have a responsibility to protect it, nourish it, and foster it in ways that we're not doing today.

Addressing problems begins with accepting and embracing the fact that you have a problem, and you have challenges, and there are issues. We don't often do that. Hence, we don't even give ourselves a chance to address these things. It's time that we begin to talk in very honest, factual, objective terms about where we are as a country so that we can start to have objective, fact-based conversations about what we can and should be doing about it and how we move forward, doing so as a collective.

And again, just because folks disagree with one another, it doesn't mean that one side is unequivocally right, and the other side is unequivocally evil.

We have to get to a place where we can have a discourse, where we can have a conversation, where we can debate in a respectful way that leads us to the best answers. As it is, we can't even talk to one another. That is not going to lead to resolving any of the issues that I just talked about.

We have to have those tough conversations. And, we have to have them in a respectful manner. We have to have them in a fashion that listens, embraces, and offers all sides a chance to voice their opinion. That doesn't mean every opinion is right or the way forward. But it does mean that those conversations can lead us to the best solution.

As a technologist, I talk to my people all the time about how innovation is not always rocket science. Instead, innovation stems from open minds and the free flow of ideas. We are not going to train bears to shake utility poles, but the idea of bears doing just that can lead to a brilliant solution.

The Canadian power company story illustrates the power of ideas. One idea may not be the answer, but if you build on that and you build on that and you build on that, a solution emerges. Before you know it, you arrive at a place that's novel, distinctive, and workable. You arrive at a place you never would have gotten to if you didn't have creative thought and diverse thinking around the table. You get to go to some fantastically interesting places.

Working Toward a Solution

There's no reason why we can't do that in our politics. There's no reason why we can't do that in our institutions. There's no reason why we can't make that a mainstay of how we move forward across all these fronts—education, social justice, incarceration, and income inequality.

All of these things need to be addressed in different and novel ways. I'm not suggesting that we don't have to work for it. This is America. People should work for what they get. In fact, it's proven that "free" is not the answer. People don't respect "free." People should be challenged. It should be hard, but it shouldn't be impossible. It should not be completely improbable. It should not be overly burdensome for a group of people. That's not who or what we are as Americans. It's not part of the ethos—first articulated by our country's founders—upon which our country was based.

Moreover, it isn't about someone taking my sliver of this American pie. It's literally about making a great pie, a big, honking pie, and getting a bigger piece of that than you otherwise would, by being inclusive and adding diverse perspectives and points of view that we currently marginalize and dismiss.

We are at a pivotal point in our journey toward that inclusive vision. In our transition to a more AI-influenced, tech-based economy and world, we are on the cusp of baking our biases into everyday life, making them a way of life. When you think about facial recognition, underwriting, access to credit, and access to capital, we risk making biased decisions a systematically permanent part of our lives. That's completely unacceptable.

We have to be better as a nation. We have to be better as a people. We have to be better as a world. We owe it to ourselves. We owe it to the very distinct gift that we've been given to be in a world, in a universe where life is unique, where life is precious and special, where life is not easy, and the prospect of it is not common.

We have a lot of work to do. I hope this effort will cause people to stop, reflect, imagine, wonder, and decide that they are going to be different.

As individuals, they are going to be different and make choices that encourage others to be different as well. In this way, we can create a movement. There is precedence for this. Nations have found their way out of conflict and injustice before. The women's suffrage movement. The civil rights movement. The end of apartheid. The European Union blossomed from the wreckage, lies, and distrust of World War II. Massive transformations of societies around eliminating inequality have happened before and need to happen again—right here, right now.

We will talk later about this coalition of the willing, the coalition of courage, and the coalition of change. And I hope the words that I'm sharing—the concepts, ideas, and thoughts—get people thinking about a coalition of like-minded people who want to move in a different direction, who understand the urgency of where we are, and who understand that we don't have all day. Time is running out.

Chapter 2

Defining the Presidency

When I think about the presidency, I think of it as a platform with a beacon. The president is there to manifest the hopes, needs, opportunities, and fortitude—not just of their constituents but of the people who didn't vote for them. As president, you are there for the whole of the country.

The presidency reminds me of the statue rising above Rio de Janeiro. That's not to say the president is a Christ figure, but the statue stands like a guardian over the people below it as if it were saying, "I'm watching out for you, I'm watching over you, I'm protecting you. If something is coming, it's going to encounter me first, and it will have to deal with me first. I'm going to have the first crack at resolving it and doing so in a manner that ensures that whatever comes next is positive for all of you."

That's how I see the platform. I see it as an opportunity to think broadly and to think differently.

I see it as a challenge, too—to get outside of your comfort zone to represent not just those who voted for you but a diverse set of perspectives, including those who did not mark your name on the ballot. Some of those perspectives may be unpopular, but you still must transcend your boundaries and barriers to lead as a president should.

Consider Lyndon B. Johnson, a Southern Democrat from Texas who never talked about the need for civil rights until he was vice president and later president. Johnson wasn't added to the ticket because of his civil rights stance; he was tapped to shore up the Southern voting bloc. But when John F. Kennedy was assassinated and Johnson became president, he knew he had to be something different. He knew he had to be something more. He knew that for the benefit of the country, both present and future, he had to carry forward a perspective he may have never harbored previously. He's one of my favorite presidents because of his compelling and courageous transformation.

Setting aside his decisions concerning the Vietnam War, Johnson's domestic accomplishments speak volumes about the kind of fortitude, foresight, and vision you must have to be president. The times we live in today and the things we're likely to experience in the future will demand that kind of capability from our president.

In July 2023, we experienced the hottest day this planet has ever recorded. This is a frightening distinction. The world is changing in ways that absolutely demand that we think differently and behave differently. We're heading down a path where correcting course and eliminating human contribution to this existential crisis will be incredibly difficult. The president needs to be the person mapping that new course—not just for the United States but for the entire world.

Having traveled all over the world, I am very conscious of the customs and cultures of different places. I don't think Americans have a lock on what's right, good, or best, but we can lead the conversations and help everyone arrive at results that are good for the vast majority of people. The platform affords the person in it and the people supporting that platform an opportunity to do those things on a very, very broad scale. When you approach those conversations with a pure heart, the best intentions, an openness, and a desire to learn, you can arrive at results and outcomes that benefit a lot of people.

There is no end to the issues we must face—whether it's climate change, income equity, social justice, or a woman's right to control what happens with her own body. Every day, people may feel powerless against problems this large. They may feel their voice would not rise above the din. They understand things are not moving in the right direction, but they don't know what to do about it.

I feel my role as president would be to help them understand that they *can* do something about it. More importantly, they have a *responsibility* to try to do something about it.

As we begin to form a coalition with these concerned people, their voice, involvement, and engagement will begin having a material impact on what's happening and the direction we're going. It reminds me of that viral video from 2009 at the Sasquatch Festival in the Columbia River Gorge in the Pacific Northwest. A young man wearing just a pair of shorts begins a free-form gyration of a dance on a grassy hillside as a reggae band jangles in the background. After a few minutes, a second man joins the first dancer, then a third. Before long scores of people are dancing, and what seemed to be an undisciplined free expression becomes a mass celebration.

Observers appreciated the first dancer's courage but noted that the movement of dozens more was triggered by the one man who joined the first and the third who joined the first two. All are valid points. However, in my mind, it started with the courage of that first person, who got out there and said, "I'm just going to live. I'm going to experience it. I'm going to do something different, something outside of the norm." And then to be joined by a second person, who others saw and said, "Maybe they're onto something." And next thing you know, you have everyone on the mountain participating in what was a very joyous and raucous kind of experience.

So that's what we're talking about. And I guess I'm that guy. I'll keep my clothes on, but I am that guy who's starting something that changes the course of life as we know it on this planet. You don't have to be the president to do that, but having that platform, that beacon, certainly helps anyone who has the conscience, courage, grace, and opportunity to effect change.

Reinventing the Wheel

I know my way around innovation. I know how to create something that has never existed before. However, I also know the value of taking things that are already out there and arranging them in novel ways to produce solutions that are radically different from what we have experienced before. Over the course of my career, I haven't reinvented the wheel.

Rather, I have used the Steve Jobs approach of taking things that exist and repurposing them in inventive ways.

Likewise, the solution to many of the problems we face is probably right in front of us. All we need to do is put those things together in ways we may not have done before.

For example, I think we should be using artificial intelligence in our judicial system to adjudicate the question of asylum. As of April 2024, there was an estimated backlog of two million asylum claims and more than one million pending cases. Meanwhile, there are less than 700 immigration judges in the country. I think there is an opportunity to leverage technology to give folks the resolution they need, one way or the other. We are never going to have sufficient time or human resources to adjudicate all of those cases in a sensible way. Technology would help us address the challenges in that space.

Steve Jobs' MP3 player, the iPod, wasn't a new invention. But the way he put that device together, utilized digital content, and organized music companies to think differently about how they licensed their music was entirely novel and changed everything. The price point, the headphones, and the sound quality all existed but had never been arranged in a package the way Jobs designed it. Ultimately, he radically changed several different industries and created new ones that didn't exist before. Sony had the Walkman and had music and video content, but at Sony, the music division couldn't talk to the hardware division, and they never put the two of them together. Sony had an opportunity to license or stream digital content before the iPod but failed to arrange the existing pieces into something revolutionary.

The answers—the opportunities—are often right in front of us. It just takes a certain pragmatism to look at what we've done, where we are, and what we have. A pinch of this, a teaspoon of that, and a dash of another thing, and voilà, we have something different. We have our answer. We have something that will make a difference. We've got something that's going to have an impact. A president can challenge people to think that way—to stop looking for manna from heaven and start looking for the jawbone of an ass.

Challenges with Our Constitutional Republic

Sometimes, I wonder if our country has outgrown its constitutional republic, our form of government. Don't get me wrong; I think our Constitution is absolutely brilliant. I am awed by how a group could have come up with things whose relevance persists the way this document has persisted. Although we all bring our own views and biases to things like fairness, there are foundational concepts in the Constitution that we can all agree with—although, in this day and age, we often disagree about even some of those foundational things.

The issues with our Constitution lie with things on the periphery of that document and the interpretation of the document. I'm talking about how our courts and lawmakers interpret the document and how we legislate around it.

For instance, consider how some Supreme Court justices take gifts and then fail to recuse themselves from cases involving the people who made the gifts. That has nothing to do with the Constitution. The Constitution doesn't explicitly forbid that, but any generally agreed-on understanding of ethical behavior would suggest that this is wrong and needs to stop. To me, it's a no-brainer. Why we debate questions like this is beyond me. A Supreme Court justice should be above reproach. If their fairness and honesty are in question, how can we not question their interpretation of this amazing document? The same holds true for Congress and the president. They must be exemplary and unblemished, but, unfortunately, they sometimes are not.

The foundation of our republic can and will endure. But how we interpret the guiding principles for our republic doesn't seem to have the same staying power or integrity as the document itself.

When I look at our constitutional amendments, I see none that I would want to overturn. But one that gives me the most consternation is the

Second Amendment—the right to bear arms. We've taken that right to some interesting places that do not seem to align with our founders' original intent.

For instance, I recently saw a shared Instagram video of an elderly man in Florida whose car was being towed from where he had illegally parked it. The car was about to be lifted when the man ran out, his gun drawn. The tow truck guy is filming him because that's what we do now. The elder is swearing and shouting, "Why are you doing this? I'm not parked here illegally." Meanwhile, the tow truck driver asks him, "Why do you have your gun drawn? Why don't you put your gun away?" The elder says, "I'm not putting it away. I'll put it in my pocket."

Is that really the kind of behavior protected by the Second Amendment? Is that what our founders intended? No, it's not. That is not what the Second Amendment was meant for. The Second Amendment gives thoughtful, reasonable, and responsible people the right to bear arms. There should be a process around our ability to ascertain how thoughtful, reasonable, and responsible a person is. I think there are ways to ascertain that, measure it, and put some governance around it to ensure these instruments are treated with the respect and responsibility they deserve.

A couple of recent Supreme Court rulings pose some intriguing potential consequences. The court's ruling on affirmative action is particularly interesting. The justices said affirmative action doesn't have an end date. Well, racism doesn't have an end date either. To suggest that we have somehow moved beyond systemic and institutional racism and bias is a fallacy. You would have to be blind, deaf, and dumb to believe that.

Likewise, many of our presidents have used executive orders to advance their agendas. Do these orders reflect the will of the people, or do they just satisfy the need of an elected leader's preferred constituency? Has that executive power been abused?

If we go back to the turn of the century when George W. Bush came into office, there was a spike in the number of executive orders. When President Obama came in, he proclaimed that he was "not going to rule by fiat" and declined to use executive orders. But he did use executive memorandums, which carry the same kind of weight and power as executive orders. In fact, his executive memos far exceeded prior administrations' executive orders, even though he boasted about using fewer directives than his predecessors.

Would I do that? I would really try to avoid doing that.

I would use a concept that Bloomberg popularized during his twelve years as mayor of New York City. Bloomberg is a billionaire, but he didn't stay in Gracie Mansion or work in Gracie Mansion. Instead, he set up his office in the same place where the city council and everybody else worked. He established an open office system. He called it the bullpen. It was a series of concentric circles, and Bloomberg and all his cabinet heads and deputies worked in the middle. Everyone had access to him. Everyone knew where the mayor was. Everyone could get on the same page. That's where Bloomberg worked for twelve years.

As president, I would do something similar. I wouldn't work in the White House but down on the Hill, right there in the chambers of Congress. We're all going to be together because we're all going to *work* together. We're going to get some stuff done. We're going to solve problems—for instance, immigration and gun violence. Now, I'm not saying I'll *never* use executive orders—those tools may be an easier way to address immigration and violence involving guns. I am, however, saying that we're going to get things done. And we are going to get this right.

We owe the country and the world the responsibility of doing our jobs. And for four years, I'm going to be there making sure we do our job. And I'm not going to let us take the easy way out by drafting an executive order to sidestep the hard questions and the hard work of addressing these issues in a comprehensive way.

It's Not About Me

I come from a family of amazingly hardworking people. From a material perspective, we came from a very humble background. But from a spiritual perspective, we were rich. We had our flaws, of course. Everyone is flawed in some way. But the things that keep me grounded are those experiences, those relatives, those memories. Everything I've accomplished has been by the grace of my family. My life is a reflection of the people who have believed in me, helped me, and supported me.

It's not about me. It's never been about me. I've never allowed it to be about me.

I had the good fortune to play college basketball, and I continue to love that sport and participate in it. I played point guard, and if you know the sport, you know that the really successful point guards distribute the ball and make the game easier for their teammates. The point guard's role is centered on getting their teammates into position, getting them unobstructed looks at the basket, getting them in favorable matchups, and then delivering them the ball at precisely the moment when they are most likely to succeed and score. For a point guard, it's all about encouragement, direction, discipline, focus, hard love, and tough love. It's all about *them*, not about *you*.

Point guards who are the focal point of scoring often don't win championships. Isaiah Thomas set the NBA on fire offensively his first couple of years, but it wasn't until he developed as a facilitator—as someone from whom things flowed—that his team, the Detroit Pistons, blossomed and won back-to-back championships from 1988 to 1990.

Steph Curry of the Golden State Warriors lights the world on fire. He is a gravitational entity because he selflessly and continuously moves without the ball. Curry doesn't handle the ball as much as many other traditional point guards, but he's constantly moving without the ball. As a dangerous scorer, his opponents chase Curry everywhere he goes, creating extraordinary opportunities for the rest of the Warriors' players. The entire floor shifts to wherever Curry goes, leaving his teammates wide open. As a result, the Warriors get plenty of easy buckets because the other team is so intensely focused on preventing Curry from beating them with thirty-foot jumpers. (He still manages to do that anyway, which is one of several reasons why the Warriors have won four championships since Curry joined the team.)

Does our president need to be a point guard? Again, I may be biased, but that analogy makes sense to me. I think the power of the presidency can be a power that corrupts, and we need someone who sees the value of creating flow and getting the ball in the right hands at the right time. We don't need someone who thinks they are the only scoring option. People who have achieved that office with the best of intentions, however flawed they may have been, have been forced to compromise and to do things they otherwise would not have done were the stakes not as high. But the temptation was too great to ignore for some. I'm not going to say that if I ever sat in that chair, I wouldn't face the same challenges and temptations. But I think one of the differences is the place from which I came and remembering why I'm there.

I'm not there for me. It's not about me. It's about everything and everyone else but me.

Chapter 3

The Gap Between Promises and Delivery

Despite the rancor and uncompromising nature of our current political climate, we all face a basic universal truth: climate change. As I write this, Death Valley in California is experiencing some of the highest temperatures ever recorded on our planet. People are flocking there to experience the incredible heat, possibly even driving their gasoline-powered cars equipped with air conditioning to find out what 128 degrees Fahrenheit feels like. At the same time, Vermont was experiencing a once-in-a-century rainstorm that left enormous swaths of the state underwater. Then, there was the record-breaking cyclone swarm in Illinois, which suffered twice as many tornadoes in 2023 than at any other time in history. From one coastline to the other, the planet is foretelling something dire and impending.

There is no debate here. Climate change is real and is happening now. By one reliable estimate, we have six years to change how we live before the damage to our planet is irreversible.

Another way to look at it is as a fork in the road. One fork is to do nothing. If you lack courage, urgency, foresight, and empathy, take that path. The other path is to accept this universal truth and act with urgency to address it. What we do next, from this point forward, will define our generation and define the life on this planet. What we do on this path defines the future of our children and all generations that follow.

Part of that universal truth is that there will be consequences. We can debate those consequences—how they bad are and how bad they will be—but we must be intentional about working on positive outcomes.

While I think it's important to review the track record of our past presidents, I don't want to attack what those presidents did. Instead, I think it's worth noting where their ideals and intentions fell short of what they wanted to achieve. I think it's also worth asking if those were the right intentions to begin with. Should they have focused less on their short-term agenda – jobs, economy, and immigration – and more on thornier, longer-term concerns? In other words, would we face such dire, existential threats today if our leaders had done more yesterday?

I understand that running for president requires that you say things, commit to things, and make promises to get elected. And once you are elected, you face more complications from lobbyists, three branches of government, interest groups, and foreign nations. All of these things obscure your target.

The Challenges

However, it feels to me that too often the ideals and promises that we start with get lost because we lack the courage, fortitude, and commitment to pursue them. There are so many other factors. "If I stand up to the NRA, what's going to happen to the rest of the party? What's going to happen to the rest of the ticket?" Never mind the senseless barrage of mass killings and shootings that happen so often that we're numb to it. There is almost an expectation that this kind of thing is going to happen every day because it *does* happen every day. And we don't seem to do anything about it.

And that is not acceptable. Mass shootings don't happen regularly anywhere else in the world. There was a mass shooting in New Zealand a couple of years ago, and the prime minister immediately reacted and ensured that weapons of that nature were no longer available. I am, by no means suggesting that we go to that extreme, but we can't just sit and do nothing either. We can't accept this as a common or acceptable way of life.

The deltas between our ideals and our outcomes need to be pointed out. I am not trying to demonize either side or any party, but we are at that fork in the road where standing pat and doing nothing is not an acceptable outcome, given the challenges we face and the risks they present. That's why I'm pledging to do whatever it takes in terms of commitment, courage, personal sacrifice, vision, outlook, work, and effort. I don't care about my legacy. I don't care about being re-elected. I care about making those four years the most impactful years possible.

And that means working literally night and day for those four years.

When my grandfather was eighty-seven, he was taken to the hospital. He had worked at U.S. Steel for over forty-five years. He was the pastor of a church he had founded. He was a carpenter, he built the sanctuary, and was engaged with his congregation, helping them, driving them, visiting them, feeding them, and fixing the homes that they lived in.

"Reverend Groce, how do you feel? What's wrong?" the doctor asked him at the hospital.

"Doctor," my grandfather said, "I'm just worn out."

That's what I expect to say at the end of my presidency. The chief White House physician will stroll into my office and ask, "How are you feeling?" And I'll tell him: "I am worn out"—by what we have done and accomplished, by all the problems we've tackled head-on, from making commitments and executing those commitments. We'll have done all those things despite the pressure, competing interests, and thorny political thickets. I'll be worn out from delivering to the people. I'll be worn out from overcoming obstacles.

Divisive Technology

At the end of the day, many of the challenges will be the same obstacles every president faces. However, I believe we are running out of time to constructively and comprehensively solve them. We talk a lot about how historically divided we are. Well, there is nothing new about that. Remember the Civil War? Have we learned nothing in the last 150 years about listening to opposing viewpoints?

The difference is that today, we are reaching a state of consciousness via the technology to which we are so connected and connected all the time. Social media has made it easy for us to flock to others who validate what we think about the world, irrespective of the accuracy or truthfulness of those thoughts and perspectives. Social media amplifies those perspectives, hardening them and giving them enhancements and persistence. As an evolving species, I don't know that humanity is currently equipped for our every thought to be an intractable public declaration that lives forever. We all have interesting thoughts, but we've never had the means to share them with millions of people for the rest of time. Yet that's exactly what we do, without really thinking, without a measure of balance, without bouncing it off a trusted advisor before hitting that send button. Is this really something I should be saying aloud? Will I feel this way tomorrow or next week or ten years from now? Do I understand the nuance of the issue? Is there more substance, context, and self-awareness I need before I make my declaration to the world?

Thus, we find ourselves in an era of divisiveness and division. Again, this is nothing new, but today, we have vitriol fueled by constant, instantaneous declarations that lack veracity and context that serve to intensify and harden our differences.

The situation makes securing positive change even more challenging. Anyone's version of truth is challenged, and this makes consensus harder and harder to reach. Without consensus, it becomes difficult and challenging to get anything done.

I'll give you a quick example of how technology is really changing things. As I write this, we recently witnessed a couple of bank failures that rattled the financial system on a global scale, starting with Silicon Valley Bank and another regional bank in California. In terms of asset size, scope, and business, both of those institutions were relatively small. But what was fascinating is how their failure was instigated through social media and the aftershock of their failures.

Some of the most influential patrons of Silicon Valley Bank essentially jumped on social media and shouted, "Get your money out now!" and within a nanosecond, you had an electronic run on the bank. It wasn't like *It's a Wonderful Life* where people stood outside the bank waiting to withdraw their money. These banks collapsed almost instantaneously.

The bank opened on Monday and was immediately drained of assets and resources—in part due to what had transpired on social media. It was the digital version of someone walking into a crowded movie theater and shouting, "Fire!" Everyone ran for the exits as fast as they could, with no questions asked or a whiff of smoke.

That's a new phenomenon. We haven't seen that before. And that contagion just continued to spread throughout the financial system. It took extraordinary measures on a global scale to stop it.

Social media tools have delivered unbelievable things—they spawned the Arab Spring, for example—but they have also damaged our trust in the world's ability to run on rational thought. They make it too easy for us to be distrustful. These tools compel us to be reactive and not reasonable and thoughtful. In the digital age, reason and rational thought often take a back seat to the latest wild allegation. This phenomenon will continue to creep into places and be a catalyst for things that we still don't understand. When you start interjecting AI into this, the possibility of creating a narrative that can spark action with grave consequences becomes even more likely.

Being Accountable

Our president must be a special kind of person who understands what these challenges are and begins to communicate and leverage them in unique and novel ways. We must begin to communicate differently. We have to touch and connect people in a different way. We have to recognize these challenges and potential threats. Can we use these tools that are creating divisiveness to actually solve some of these problems and create a common sense of purpose? Can we create a shared model of universal truths and goodwill that assures people that we are coming from a place of good intentions and that we are going to give each other some measure of grace? We need to create a narrative that says it's okay to have a different perspective.

I don't have all the answers. Nor do I think my answers are the only answers. I am, however, not going to demonize someone who has a different perspective. It's okay to think differently. It is critical that somewhere in all of the morass of thoughts and views that we have on issues, we find that kernel of truth, that kernel of commonality, that will allow us to move forward and do something constructively good to alleviate the challenges of the situations and circumstances that we currently face.

This is a different element of the presidency that has to be recognized for the good, not the bad. I think that our prior president stumbled on leveraging this technology, creating a narrative that fit his designs and objectives irrespective of whether it was the truth or not. He weaponized falsehoods, inaccuracies, and half-truths. That's dangerous. He showed how these tools can be used for objectives that don't solve things in a constructive way. Now we must recognize these tools for the power they have and the importance they play.

Accountability is critical. For example, when I asked my parents how to handle certain problems, they responded with questions and not answers. They wanted me to develop an ability to solve problems and make decisions, so I had to figure it out for myself. They didn't tell me what to do, but they held me accountable for the decisions I made. Years later, my father told me that he was trying to create in me and my siblings a sense of critical thinking. In this way, he could guide me from a place of ignorance about what I should do to a place of self-confidence where I could say, "Here is what I'm going to do."

The Parable of the Talents from the Book of Matthew tells the story of a man who, prior to a long journey, entrusts his wealth to his servants. One servant receives five talents, a second gets two, and a third gets one. The first two servants invest their talents and double their money. The third one buries his talent in a hole, afraid of losing the money he has been given. When the man returns, he praises his first two servants but admonishes the third for being fearful and unproductive. The point of the parable is to symbolize the concept of using and multiplying the gifts we are given, including those from God, and encouraging people to make use of their talents. That was the basis on which I was raised.

We had to do something. We had to figure out what that something was, and we were held accountable for what we did—including inaction unless inaction was the right answer. For the most part, though, doing nothing was not acceptable. Doing something was half the battle. And doing the right thing was the ultimate right answer. The only way we avoided punishment was to figure something out, do something, and get it right.

And so, I've lived a life of accountability. I lived a life of doing something. I can't sit still.

What Did *You* Do?

I cannot simply sit and observe what is unfolding and say nothing and do nothing, and not be accountable for using my talent. There is going to be a reckoning, and someone's going to ask me, "What did you do?" The answer can't be nothing.

And so, it is for the office of the presidency. A president has four years to impact this country. Four years to impact lives. Four years to impact life on this planet. The answer can't be, "Well, Congress wouldn't let me," or "The Supreme Court wouldn't let me," or "Lobbyists and special interests stood in my way." The answer can't be that, especially given where we are, that fork in the road, where doing nothing is going to lead to something catastrophic, and doing something could lead to something glorious—the start of something big. Maybe not all the right answers, but at least the answers that push us along the path toward success.

I often think of myself as existing above this abyss, caught between something more and nothing at all. I can't go back to nothing at all. I've got to keep moving forward to something more, irrespective of how foggy, treacherous, or tenuous that path may be. I've got to keep moving towards something more.

There are extraordinary challenges on the road ahead. Unique challenges.

Ray Kurzweil, a globally recognized computer scientist, inventor, and futurist, talks about how, in the near future, AI and technological advancement will bring about profound changes to civilization. According to Mr. Kurzweil, technology is advancing at an exponential rate and will surpass human intelligence, leading to almost incomprehensible advancements in medicine, energy, and computing. For example, he predicts that soon, blood-cell-sized devices known as nanobots will be injected inside our bodies and will fight diseases and improve our memory and cognitive abilities. He gives an example in his book, *The Singularity Is Near*, of lily pads on a pond. You look at it every day and it just doesn't seem to change. But if you go away and return after a time, the entire pond is covered with lily pads. It's 2 times 2 is 4, 4 times 4 is 16, and so on. Exponential growth. That's what is happening with technology.

Today, technology seems to be dividing us. Tomorrow, it could unite us. But it's going to take someone who understands that and leverages it for that purpose.

Technology for Good

When Apple, Google, or Disney want to get their message out about a new product, their use of technology and social media tools is masterful.

Our government must operate in that same way. It has to be a 24/7 assault that is never-ending, quick, and everywhere.

We're poised to put people on Mars. We just built and deployed an observation platform in deep space, the James Webb Telescope. We can do extraordinary things as a species, as a world, and certainly as a country. We have to recognize these advancements for what they are and lean into them a thousand percent. We have to be masters of it. We have to be the best. For example, back in World War II, our government leveraged Hollywood to sell the message about what we were doing, the righteousness of our pursuits in World War II. That needs to be resurrected in a different form for a different time, for a different purpose.

But we can't allow the people who would leverage these tools for lies and deception to continue unabated. We can't approach the problem in a half-hearted way and hope people find the truth. We can't hope that people will discover the truth on their own.

We have to be as committed to our side of the story as those folks who spread half-truths and outright lies are to theirs.

We are going to build this coalition of the willing. We are going to build this coalition of two and three, and we are going to continue to add to it. We will be steadfastly dedicated to the truth and intensely devoted to our story, just as they appear to be to theirs. The difference is that truth endures.

Speaking of these tools, it is interesting how they are constructed and deployed. And it is worth understanding the purposes that they serve.

In the film *The Princess Bride*, Inigo Montoya, a skilled swordsman seeking revenge against the six-fingered man who killed his father, is played by Mandy Patinkin. Inigo is working with Vizzini, played by Wallace Shawn, and Vizzini keeps using the word "inconceivable" to describe events happening around them. Whenever something unexpected occurs, Vizzini exclaims, "Inconceivable!" Finally, Inigo turns to Vizzini and says, "You keep using that word. I do not think it means what you think it means." This iconic line has become memorable due to Inigo's calm yet humorous correction of Vizzini's misuse of the term "inconceivable."

My point is, I don't think these tools are what people think they are. I don't think they are used for the purposes that people think they are being used. In that sense, the president and the people working with the president must understand these tools for what they are and lean into them really hard—really, really hard.

Chapter 4

The Power of Unity

In the late 1990s, astronomers and space agencies from several countries began discussing the need to replace the Hubble Telescope. Hubble's ability to study certain wavelengths, particularly in the infrared spectrum, was limited, and space explorers from various countries saw the value of a new telescope better equipped to gather light and see through cosmic dust clouds to study the formation of stars and galaxies.

Thus was born the idea for the James Webb Space Telescope, a large, space-based observatory designed to revolutionize our understanding of the cosmos. More than thirty years after the idea for a new platform was hatched, scientists from NASA, the European Space Agency, and the Canadian Space Agency launched the JWST from French Guiana on Christmas Day in 2021. Almost miraculously, the delicate device was hurtled into space to a position about a million miles from Earth, where it unfolded and employed a large sun shield that enabled researchers around the globe to study the formation of galaxies, stars, and planetary systems. Scientists could study atmospheres on exoplanets and examine the mysteries of dark matter and dark energy.

The James Webb platform boggles my mind—in more ways than one. While it provides opportunities for us to explore the early universe and perhaps reveal new details about cosmic history after the Big Bang, it also represents the magic that occurs when people work with a united sense of purpose.

A Shared Model of Success

Over the course of my life—everywhere I turn and everywhere I look—I see the significance of people coming together for a common cause. I have seen people joining forces, creating collectives and a shared sense of purpose—this shared mental model of success.

When people selflessly blend their capabilities and talents, the things that they're capable of—both good and bad—are just absolutely extraordinary. When you have that purposeful blending, where people understand purpose, division, mission, and objectives, and are committed, focused, and disciplined about getting something done, you can reach astonishing heights or unimaginable lows.

Even before the James Webb project, we had examples of people uniting around the idea of exploring space. When President John F. Kennedy announced in the early 1960s that we were going to go to the moon by the end of the decade, you could almost hear and imagine the gasp that went out. *But that's not possible. There's no way. By the end of the decade, it's never going to happen.* Yet it did. Even after Kennedy was gone, forces had been galvanized by that declaration and came together and made that happen.

Moreover, the world is full of those kinds of achievements. We see it in sports, science, politics, and economics. We are constantly bombarded by examples of people doing things in situations of catastrophic events. Hurricane Katrina jumps to mind; something extraordinarily devastating happened and people—good people, normal people, irrespective of what the government did or didn't do and various other impediments—came together and helped their neighbor. That sense of community that evolves and rises up out of that kind of situation is powerful.

What we have to do, and what I'm hoping this book does, is help people create that sense of purpose, that sense of commonality, that brings them to the realization that at the end of the day, we are all on the same page. We all want the same things. We all have the same concerns and needs. In many cases, our struggles are similar in nature, and the solutions to these challenges can be born out of a collective. It's born out of unity. It comes from a willingness to, again, selflessly sacrifice towards a unified goal and common sense of purpose.

I think of it as a kind of hive. A colony. A highly integrated collective where everyone understands that purpose. Everyone understands that vision. Moreover, everyone understands their role, the importance of the role, and the contribution that their role makes to the overall end goal we're trying to accomplish.

I had a leader once who talked about everyone playing their position. Think of a baseball team where all nine players are stationed in various places for a reason. When they all play their position—they all play their roles, understand their role, and submit to the responsibility of playing the roles—the team succeeds. People work together, irrespective of whether their role is front and center or gets all the glory. Everybody understands that their role is crucial to achieving the goal.

That's how I think about unity.

I also understand unity is a double-edged sword. It can be used for purposes that are, well, less pure. Perhaps even for evil. It happens, and we must be alert to this and ensure that we're all on the same page and that the collective remains centered on purity, integrity, and good intentions.

That said, it is all well and good to intend something, to dream of something. But at the end of the day, it has to result in something. It has to bring about something that is as pure as our intentions. It's got to align with our objectives.

We've all seen situations where that doesn't happen. Unfortunately, we see it a lot in politics; we intend many things but sometimes wind up in a place far from where we intended. It has to start with something, and it has to start with someone. There must be a catalyst, a spark. But that spark, whoever or whatever that is, can't allow itself to be the centerpiece. This is not about a cult. It's not about a cult of personality.

It's about building a collective. It's about creating unity. That spark quickly grows into a flame. It never stands out from the flame. It can never be differentiated from the flame. And when that happens, you give yourself a chance to make something extraordinary happen.

Our Divisions Are Deepening

When I think about the current political polarization, I feel nothing can surprise me anymore. Certainly, I've seen the worst of it, right?

Wrong.

Seemingly every day, a new, and utterly bewildering headline emerges, surpassing the prior day's audacity. For example, the Board of Education in Florida ratified a new curriculum that teaches young people that Black slaves learned beneficial skills they could use for their own benefit. It is extremely difficult to fathom what "benefits" are implied here and that it took subjugation to impart that knowledge. What kind of skills were those? How to drain swamps? Cut sugar cane? Extracting pine resin for turpentine? In short, how to endure grueling dehumanizing physical work that damages people psychologically? How you can make the argument that slaves benefited in any way from their bondage is preposterous. But that's what Florida students will learn. Who concocts such ideas and proclaims them as educational? Who thinks these things are good ideas?

Our societal fissures are deepening, evolving from faint dotted lines that become dashes and then morph into formidable chasms that threaten to engulf us. There are moments when the impulse to cry out in disbelief is overwhelming. It makes you want to run outside and just scream at the top of your lungs. "Wake up! Wake up! What are we doing?"

It makes you want to confront the architects of division and question their vision, asking, "What is the end goal? What is the end state? Is this not the opposite of the unity we're trying to drive toward?"

What is the intended outcome of all this divisiveness and divisive actions? What is the benefit? And to what end will it all serve? How is that going to make life better? How is that going to make our ability to care for our families and our loved ones better?

What is the logic and the objectives they are trying to achieve? It astounds me that these divisions not only exist, but they persist. Moreover, they are growing in ways that feel almost exponential in nature.

It fills me with an acute sense of urgency and a desperate desire to instigate change. We must do something. Something has to change. There must be a spark.

We need a catalyst.

Whatever that is or whomever that is, something must be done. Without intervention, the path we are on leads nowhere promising for any of us.

Issues to Address

On the other hand, benefits and opportunities arise from unity.

As a country, there are basic, fundamental things we need to get done. Care for our elderly. Care for our children. Care for different groups within our mosaic.

Consider the hotly contested and highly contentious issue of abortion rights and some of the subsequent policies that have emerged; policies that incentivize individuals to betray the privacy and choices of others. It begs the question: Who genuinely believes these are beneficial strategies? I am not advocating abortion. I am, however, opposed to inciting people to rat out those who may have gotten an abortion. Again, who thinks that is a good idea?

Look at our nation's children and their education. The pandemic may have cost us a generation of children who have been left behind in their math and reading scores. The educational system, operating, by some standards, sub-optimally before the pandemic, was notably impacted by the pandemic, and the resulting issues may have placed an entire generation at a disadvantage. The pre-existing disparities in math and reading skills have been profoundly amplified and exacerbated, with the digital and income divide widening along demographic lines, further limiting access to vital resources for learning.

The surge in homelessness is a complex, nuanced, and persistent problem exacerbated by the pandemic. What are the root causes? Is it mental illness, systemic bias around jobs, or the lack of affordable housing? It could be any of these things, a combination of all of these things, and dozens of other causes on top of these issues.

Unity could help us think differently about these problems as well as the possible opportunities. Almost certainly, the homelessness problem, which for many is a constant, visual reminder of our inability as a society to take care of its members, will require collaboration. It will require public-private partnerships, prevention and education, living wages, and employment opportunities, be they in public or private settings. Seriously, if we are capable of rocketing a delicate telescope a million miles into space, doesn't the homeless problem seem like something we could successfully address? What is certain is that inaction will not resolve this or any other societal ailment.

Our country's unique struggle with mass shootings is yet another grievous problem that persists without a unified effort to find a resolution. It is peculiar to our culture and country, and we have allowed it to persist. While safeguarding individual rights is paramount, a consensus-driven approach could pave the way to some sustainable solutions and safety. Instead, we've normalized these tragedies by failing to do anything meaningful to stop them from occurring. As a result, mass shootings have become a common part of our everyday lives.

Centuries from now, historians may well scrutinize this era with profound perplexity and bewilderment, questioning our collective inertia. They'll ponder why solutions eluded a society that had every resource at its disposal. They will ask, "What were they thinking? What were they doing? Why couldn't they come together and fix this sooner? And what was the catastrophic damage done by just allowing situations such as these to persist and carry on for elongated periods of time, with no action, vision, courage, or sense of urgency, and no demonstrative intention to do something, to fix something, or to make something better?" The narrative doesn't have to be one of inaction and regret but can also be a testament to our collaborative spirit in addressing and overcoming adversity. It's not about assigning blame or declaring one perspective as the absolute truth;

the answers to these and other problems lie somewhere in the middle ground, in a space where compromise and collaboration can flourish.

Ultimately, unity stands as the cornerstone of our future prosperity. It is through our collective spirit that we will find our redemption. Together, there is nothing we can't do, there is no problem we can't solve, and there is no challenge we can't overcome. Should we succumb to the false dichotomy of "us versus them," we risk not just stagnation but the very foundations of our society. The path to salvation, to progress, is paved with unity—embracing the idea that together, we are stronger.

Dark Optimism

I am wary of sounding overly dramatic or pessimistic. The truth is that these challenging and contentious issues do have the potential to catalyze unity. To bridge the divides, irrespective of the issue at hand, it is imperative that all parties come together in the spirit of cooperation. Gun rights activists don't support mass shootings. The simplistic solution of confiscating all firearms only serves to alienate them, potentially rendering them obstinate. To those weary of the violence, the path forward involves engaging gun owners constructively, inviting them to collaborate on finding viable solutions. It's about replacing condemnation with goodwill and seeking a consensual, unified approach to address this and other pressing challenges.

Until we can find the courage and the wherewithal to focus on these things that way, we are in a perilous place and on a perilous path.

Long ago, I began describing myself as a dark optimist. It is my nature to see reasons for hope, but I view that hope through a veil that represents our struggle as humans.

I struggled with depression for most of my life. I had a very challenging childhood. As I mentioned earlier, my parents (particularly my father) were tiger parents on steroids. Their expectations and demands for excellence were out of this world, and they were unrelenting about my siblings and I achieving success. In some cases, their expectations felt unattainable, and failure had serious repercussions.

My father was not shy about that. Although brilliant, he had the capacity to be an intensely angry person. Often, when he came home from work, my brother, sisters, and I would scatter. We would hide until we could ascertain whether our father was angry and, if so, how angry. You did not want to be in his presence when he was angry, and he was very often angry.

This was the start of my depression.

I was never quite enough, and his harsh upbringing seemed to inform his treatment of us. Despite my high intelligence, my father often referred to me as something opposite. He did it to drive and motivate me, and I suppose on many levels, he succeeded. This interaction fostered some deep-seated anger and some enduring feelings of doing whatever it took to prove that nothing was beyond my ability.

This feeling of not being enough—of not measuring up—fuels me to this day.

Somewhere along the line, I internalized those feelings. Regardless of my accomplishments, I felt inside that I was not enough, that I missed the mark and could have and should have done better. I battle that sense of irrelevance every day.

Consequently, a sense of darkness follows me. It is a vital part of me. It fuels and drives me. I do want to be clear that my emotional state is one hundred percent my responsibility and no one except me is accountable for what and how I feel.

That said, optimism is my guiding light. I once read somewhere that "man is born with the gift of hope eternal." I soldier on, constantly seeking the silver linings hidden within the darkest clouds, believing that despite the immense challenges and daunting probabilities, redemption and success remain attainable outcomes. I maintain a sense of hope: if I can get through one more minute, I will come out the other side, improved, better, and more capable. That notion has bred in me an enduring persistence, a willingness, and an ability to keep pushing through that dark curtain to the warmth and sunshine on the other side.

I remember a sermon my paternal grandmother gave one Sunday in our church when I was very young. I don't remember the details but I remember the central theme. It caused me to sit up in the pew. Her message stopped me in my tracks.

She spoke about times in her life when she felt like she'd just hit a wall and couldn't go forward after facing what appeared to be insurmountable obstacles. "In those moments, I find myself praying that I'm not going to stop. I am not going surrender, yield, or go backward. I'm going to march in place until I can find a way to move forward." That image she painted has never faded from my memory and is still vivid in my mind to this day.

I am optimistic about life. I'm always looking for silver linings because I believe they exist even in the darkest times. However, I brace myself for the inevitable complications—we're bound to falter, to place obstacles in our own way, obscuring and complicating the path while entangling the intentions associated with getting to those silver linings. Nevertheless, I am unwavering in my belief: we will reach our destination. I am resoundingly optimistic about that. However, we won't get there without some pain, unfortunate drawbacks, deviations, roadblocks, and detours along the way.

The dark optimist says we will arrive, but only after we've acknowledged and courageously addressed the most complicated elements of our journey. The essence of dark optimism is not just surviving but thriving through adversity. And while I may be part of the spark that illuminates our path, the true light comes from the unity and collective courage of us all.

Don't get me wrong. I see the need for the spark, and I feel compelled to be that spark. Yet, this journey is not about any single individual. It never is and never will be. And I'm not even sure it *is* me. In some regards, I hope it's not. In that sense, I pray as Jesus prayed, "Let this cup pass from me."

In actuality, it's about us, collectively. I absolutely will be part of the unified effort that fearlessly addresses our world's issues with intention and resolve. It's about doing something meaningful, refusing to succumb to a narrative of despair. We are going to do something. We are going to address these things. We are not going to allow them to persist and create this sense of hopelessness.

Moments of Unity

Americans have witnessed the formidable force of unity on many momentous occasions. The Civil Rights Movement, galvanized by Dr. Martin Luther King Jr., serves as a testament to the moral fortitude of a people united. An extraordinary number of people vehemently opposed King's work, but it's clear that folks in King's movement were on the right side of history. Despite the significant strides made, the legacy of King's dream is a continued journey—one that reminds us of our collective responsibility to further the cause of justice and equality, even decades after his untimely death. However, the power of the unity he created, and the persistence of that power are evident. Because it was relentless and pure, it ultimately had a profound impact.

The days after 9/11 were another time of great unity. I was at my job in New York City that day and watched the second plane hit the tower. At that moment, my colleagues and I knew this had to be an intentional act.

This was a horrific event, and the days that followed were dark. As the smoke cleared from the rubble of the Twin Towers, a spirit of cooperation and collective strength prevailed. These were hateful acts that triggered hateful responses, dissent, and unfounded theories about what had happened and why. But at the same time, we saw unity. We saw people pulling together, and we saw New York City unified. People from all over the country sent their support. Volunteers lined up to help clear the mess. The American flag flew tall, proud, and strong in the weeks and months that followed. From this ghastly act, many Americans came to understand both the vulnerability and the power of our country, and that understanding united us. Were we able to harness that sense of unity, sustain it, and tackle more problems with it? Sadly, I'm not sure we utilized that fusion of support and purpose for all the good things we could have accomplished. A crisis will often draw us together, but we need to ensure that unity is used with the purest intention because only then can we create something good.

There's an old saying, "Never let a good crisis go to waste." This phrase, whether originating from Winston Churchill or adapted by leaders like Nelson Mandela, encapsulates the often-profound opportunities that exist within calamity. Mandela's response to apartheid's brutal division illustrated how extraordinary reform can emerge from the ashes of strife.

The Challenge Ahead

So, how do you foster unity in a diverse and polarized society where people hold strongly opposed views?

The crawl-walk-run approach is the way to go. We must start by crawling.

Unity might be a quick byproduct after a terrorist attack or the bombing of a naval installation in Pearl Harbor. But it's a struggle for us to unify in times when we don't face an existential threat.

We're going to have to learn something new, and we have to relentlessly pursue that knowledge. It's going to require an everyday focus, seven days a week, twenty-four hours a day. We need people committed to creating unity, be it for a cause, a set of objectives, a vision, or a mission. We need people who keep driving and never let it go.

One of my favorite stories from the Bible comes from Genesis, when Jacob, returning to Canaan to meet his brother, Esau, gets into a wrestling match with a man one night while alone by the Jabbok River. Some interpretations suggest this mysterious man was actually an angel of God. In any case, Jacob and the man struggled all night until, near dawn, the man dislocated Jacob's hip. Jacob continued to wrestle, demanding a blessing from the man. The man eventually blessed Jacob, renaming him Israel, which means "he who struggles with God" or "God strives." The name change symbolized Jacob's new identity and his transformation as one who perseveres and contends with God.

We have to come at our own challenges with that level of relentlessness.

When I played college basketball, we observed a ritual known as Midnight Madness. Lefty Driesell, the venerable basketball coach at the University of Maryland, created this practice. Here's how it worked:

The NCAA had a rule that college teams could not begin practice until October 15. So, in 1971, Driesell organized an event at Maryland's Cole Field House where his team would start practice the second the clock struck midnight, the earliest moment that teams could begin their preseason. Driesell opened the gym to students, fans, and the media, generating publicity and excitement about the upcoming season.

Over time, Midnight Madness became a celebratory event, with music, entertainment, player introductions, and activities for fans. Soon, other universities were adopting the practice, and it became an ESPN event, with Midnight Madness at Duke, the University of North Carolina, and other schools, including the one I played basketball for—Boston University under coach Rick Pitino also had Midnight Madness. And, if you know Rick Pitino, you know how intense he can be. Midnight Madness at BU was, indeed, total madness. We were like rabid dogs going after it on the court that night.

Imagining a presidential term that embodies this spirit, I see the inauguration not as a singular event but as a kickoff to a tenure marked by tireless endeavor. I envision my inauguration and subsequent term being an extended version of Midnight Madness. I visualize my inauguration taking place on Wall Street at the same site where George Washington was inaugurated. I picture myself and members of my cabinet running up Broadway to a waiting helicopter that whisks us off to the White House, where we immediately get to work.

I'm not waiting for a televised event that happens on Inauguration Day. I want to be sworn in at 12:01 a.m. and start work immediately.

We are rolling up our sleeves. We're getting the work. And we won't stop working until that clock strikes twelve o'clock on the 20th of January, four years later.

That's the sense of purpose, urgency, and commitment that we're going to have.

We'll work to overcome all of the divisiveness, the interest groups, and everybody seemingly pulling in a different direction. We'll help the country understand that we're not striving for different things. The views of how we reach our goals may be different. The perspectives on the road we should take may be different. But at the end of the day, we want and need the same things.

We can find common ground. There are enough commonalities between the things we need and the things we want and the roads that we have to take to get there.

That's what my administration will be centered on. We're going to crawl, then walk, and then we're going to run—with relentlessness and precision that will not stop.

This is not a journey for personal legacy; it is a selfless marathon toward a collective goal. At its conclusion, worn from the rigors of leadership, the baton will be passed to the next generation of leaders, now ready to continue the relentless pursuit of what is right and what is just, empowered by the example of dedication they've witnessed. I'm not worried about any sort of personal legacy. By the end of four years, I am going to be "worn out." Completely "worn out."

The essence of this endeavor is to demonstrate integrity and the strength of pure intent, crafting an environment where emerging leaders are emboldened to act with conviction and clarity. It is my desire to cultivate a legacy of courageous leadership, akin to the storied tenacity of Mandela or the foundational stewardship of Washington. We will groom the next group of selfless leaders as we create an example of what courageous governance looks like. We will show the people what purity of thought and intentions look like, such that a new set of leaders can fearlessly rise up with conviction about what the right thing is and be armed with the skills to do the right thing in the right way.

We will turn it over to them, and they will get after it. And I get to go lay on a beach somewhere.

Getting There

What are some of the hurdles we'll face in achieving this vision of unity?

To understand the enormous labyrinth of social fractures, we must recognize that the tendrils of division have harnessed social media as an incredibly compliant and fertile ground to sow discord. The powers of division have become amazingly effective at utilizing social media to create a story, tell a story, and simply make up narratives where a story doesn't exist. They use social media to buttress their point of view and whatever objectives they're trying to achieve, even if those objectives are just focused on sowing chaos. Our world, so vivid in its cultural tapestry, finds itself marred by enduring rifts across racial, gender, religious, and political lines – a dissonance that, perplexingly, we not only inherit but also actively perpetuate.

The lines of division are all over the place. For example, we continue to be divided by race.

Our society's richness lies in its diverse plurality. It is a prime ingredient of our secret sauce. That plurality doesn't exist anywhere else in the world – a characteristic of our country that is unique on the global stage. And because we have it, we are empowered to do things that belie our size. We're able to innovate beyond the capabilities of other more populous nations.

Countries with over a billion people can't invent the things that we invent. They can't create the things that we create. They can't do the things that we do. This diversity should be our unifying strength, not the fault lines of our undoing.

Even where the lines of division don't exist, we create them. We have lines around gender, race, religion, and partisanship. It boggles the mind where these lines exist and how they persist. Even within groups, we have lines. You know, in the AfricanAmerican community, the color of our skin within our community is a line. Are you kidding me? That's ridiculous. We have lines around class and economic division. There's a line between north and south in this country that persists.

I remember wanting to hire a brilliant young man from the South for my New York City-based bank. Some of my colleagues, however, did not share my enthusiasm for the candidate.

"I don't think he's smart," one of the hiring managers said. "The way he talks. I don't think he's all that smart."

"Are you serious?" I replied, incredulous. Because the applicant was from the southern suburbs and talked with a bit of a twang, he was perceived by us New York City hustlers as being maybe a tad slow. I did hire the individual, and he performed every bit as brilliantly as I thought he would.

We must overcome lines like this with honesty, acknowledgment, transparency, and curiosity. We must ask, "Why is there a line here? What's the point of it? What do we get out of it, and what do we do with it?" Those are questions for people who choose to exist on one side of that line or another.

That is how we must challenge those lines and demand they be erased. Acknowledge their pointlessness and negativity, and once done, let's eliminate them. Let's choose a different path.

You do that step, by step, by step, by step.

And eventually, we'll get there.

Chapter 5

Defining the Agenda for Change

When I lived in New York City, I loved going to Washington Square Park, where people often gather to play chess. In the park, the rules require each player to make their move within thirty seconds of their opponent's move. Anyone who plays chess understands how difficult that is. At any given point in a chess match, there are probably a million different moves you *could* make and about ten different moves you *should* make to support your strategy. And you have only thirty seconds to decide the one move that does the job best. You have to act quickly, even though you're asking the human mind to do something that isn't natural. The mind prefers analysis over instinct. But these Washington Square Park matches leave little time for analysis.

Politics is different. When you're looking at politics as a citizen who wants elected officials to do something, it often feels like they are stuck in an endless loop of analysis that never reaches the point of execution. The chess pieces never move, or else they move in a timid or safe manner. The slow shuffle of pieces across the board is immensely frustrating to constituents, who yearn to see bold and decisive action rather than tentative or cautious play.

Those of us who get up and work every day don't have that option. Sure, we evaluate and analyze, but getting something done is crucial to our success. It's like that at every step of the corporate ladder. At J.P. Morgan, we had a saying, "Execution is king." We weren't alone in that philosophy. As Jamie Dimon once said, "Hope is not a strategy." Likewise, *trying* is not a strategy. Dreams and visions are nothing more than dreams and visions without execution. You have to get things done.

Politics, meanwhile, involves a lot of talking. A *lot* of talking, negotiating, influencing—often at the expense of execution.

This concept of swift and decisive execution is what I intend to bring to the presidential office. The complexities of governance are undeniable, with countless possible moves and unforeseen challenges at every turn. Yet, it is critical to distill this complexity into actionable agendas, focusing on a core set of priorities that ripple through the vast ocean of policy matters. As president, there might be a million different moves you can make and a thousand more issues that come up while you're in office. That's expected. But to execute and accomplish something from the get-go, you need to focus on the three to five things that are connected to a myriad of other things. They are interconnected threads in the fabric of our society, each one impacting the other, intertwining in a complex weave that requires a strategic and holistic approach. In my mind, those issues include immigration, climate change, gun violence, and technology.

Immigration

Immigration is not just an immigration issue; it's also an economic issue.

Most of the Western world, including the United States, is getting older. A large percentage of the workforce is reaching retirement age, and that has a direct impact on economic stability, viability, growth, and economic welfare. As older workers leave their jobs, fewer people are left to work, produce goods and services, and support the benefits needed by all these retired citizens. The situation is exacerbated by declining birth rates juxtaposition higher life expectancy rates.

Can the answer to this equation be immigration? The United States was built on immigration. We have a big statue sitting in New York Harbor. It is a symbol of freedom and democracy. At its base is a plaque that reads:

> "Give me your tired, your poor,
> Your huddled masses yearning to breathe free,
> The wretched refuse of your teeming shore.
> Send these, the homeless, tempest-tost to me,
> I lift my lamp beside the golden door!"

Everyone in every corner of the globe knows something about the American Dream. Our nation's fabric—its very genesis and growth—has been colored by the dreams and toils of immigrants. The U.S. narrative is woven with immigrant threads, symbolized by Lady Liberty's enduring call in New York Harbor. This heritage is not merely our past; it's our blueprint for future prosperity. Embracing immigration, when constructed legally and thoughtfully, is essential. If we are going to continue to grow and prosper, we need immigration. We need constructive immigration. We need legal immigration. We need immigration, and we need to figure it out.

To streamline this process, we must revisit the original intent and the classic definition of asylum, while integrating technology for efficiency. Imagine artificial intelligence rapidly parsing through the backlog of immigration cases, informed by decades of judicial decisions. That will serve as our first line of adjudication for the vast majority of these cases. This blend of tradition and innovation could revolutionize our approach, moving us beyond the stalemate of our current system. Then, we can go about enforcement.

I am a proponent of immigration and always will be. I don't believe our system is broken or irrevocably damaged. However, it must be significantly altered, and it demands thoughtful, strategic modification. What we're doing today isn't working, and it's not going to work. It's not a question of simply trying harder; we need to rethink the game and evolve.

Gun Violence: An Unacceptable Normalcy

Every administration in recent years has talked about gun control. But it's just talk. Real action is set aside because it's just too hard.

I don't care if it's hard. We need to tackle this issue head-on from day one. People should be able to feel safe.

Consider Chicago, where the website heyjackass.com starkly illustrates the crisis. You would never know by the name, but this website is phenomenal in a very morbid way: the site meticulously records shootings, neighborhood by neighborhood, detailing the human cost with an almost sardonic precision. An infographic charts gunshots to the head, torso, arms, and lower body.

It tracks gunshot deaths as well as stabbings (gunshot deaths accounted for 90 percent of deaths in 2023, and stabbings accounted for 4 percent).

The site maps the shooting deaths, exposing which parts of Chicago are relatively safe and thriving and which parts have been decimated by violence, literally a war zone. You can see which schools are affected and which neighborhoods are unsafe. There is a devastating statistical thoroughness belied by a faint undertone of scornful mockery, characterized by the site's name (Hey Jackass!) and its tagline ("Illustrating Chicago Values"). You can even buy T-shirts and other swag featuring the site's distinctive chalk outline of a shooting victim.

The violence goes on day after day after day, with mass shootings you never hear about.

And this is happening just as a normal course of business.

As I write this, someone in Chicago is shot every two hours and forty-six minutes. A person is murdered every thirteen hours and twenty-eight minutes. That's absolutely insane. It should not be tolerated.

I recall thinking that Columbine was the worst we would ever get. But then came Virginia Tech, Sandy Hook, Parkland, Mandalay Bay, and on and on.

I get how difficult this topic is. These shootings may seem like isolated events, but they trigger a cascade effect. In a place like Chicago, gun violence affects the educational system, the economic system, and public services. Police and courts are stretched. Municipal services are curtailed or disrupted. Schools can start to feel unsafe, which can't be helping children learn. If we can control and curtail the violence, life improves for everyone.

The same is true with immigration. If we get that under control, we can have vibrant, amazing immigration into this country. We'll have more workers and less debilitating paperwork for employers. We'll have more tax revenue. We'll have more diverse classrooms and the brilliant ideas that emerge from those circumstances.

Climate Change

To get climate change under control, we must invest in renewable energy sources. That's going to be the future, like it or not, want it or not. People right now have the ability to install solar panels on their roofs and eliminate or at least minimize their dependence on utility power, which all too often is generated from coal-burning plants. The problem for most is the upfront cost. Why do we expect our citizens to make these significant financial sacrifices to wean themselves from a wasteful utility grid? Isn't there more our government can do to help people beyond the paltry tax credits we offer?

Addressing climate change is a national imperative. It's imperative to our way of life. It's imperative to our defenses. It's imperative to our educational system. To dawdle, to fail to lead, innovate, and invest is to contribute to our demise.

We are going to come in on day one with a plan. We're going to listen to a lot of folks, getting views and perspectives on what these priorities should be. Then, we're going to solve them in a way that's different from previous efforts.

Returns on Investment

Think of solving these problems as a return on investment, or ROI.

What's the ROI of gun violence? What's the ROI of climate change? What's the ROI of immigration? And by that, I mean, how many more benefits do we create by addressing this particular core issue? Using this ROI perspective to determine our priorities will help us make better decisions about the three to five things that we should start with to drive the most dramatic, lasting, far-reaching change that we can within our country and within the world.

That's how I'm going to think about it. That's how I think about what I do every single day. What's the greatest return on investment? What's the greatest benefit that I can derive from the efforts that I put forward? How do I ensure that I'm protecting shareholder equity, protecting a team, creating team member value, and creating value for our customers with the work I'm doing?

Again, there are a million things we could do. There are a million things we *should* do. But there are ten things we *can* do that create the greatest value and the greatest return on the limited resources that we have at our disposal to get things done.

A crucial piece of this is how we tell our story. We need to craft our message, perspective, vision, and mission in the form of a story. Effective communication wields great impact.

Tiger Woods once talked about how he would know he'd arrived as a professional golfer (perhaps the best golfer in history) when he "owned" his swing. I can't play a lick of golf, but I understood what he meant. When Woods—in any situation, any time, under any condition, under any circumstances—needed his swing, he could recreate it because he owned it. It was a part of his DNA. I am god-awful at golf. My swing has been banned in all fifty states, but I could relate it to basketball, something I play very well. In basketball, I own my shot. I can create my shot irrespective of time, opponent, distance, or circumstances. I can get to my spot, and I can create my shot.

In the same way, we have to own our story. That's how I think about communication. Humans understand storytelling. They understand a great story. That's why we need to craft our message and our perspective, our vision, and our mission in the form of a story.

Robert Kennedy told stories. Martin Luther King Jr. told stories. King often used personal anecdotes from his own life to humanize the struggle for civil rights and to connect with his audience. King became more personal, memorable, and understandable through the stories he told. He also used allegories, metaphors, and biblical fables, which engrossed his predominantly religious audiences. He shared stories of courage, resilience, and nonviolent protest to create a shared vision with his adherents in their fight for civil rights. He used stories to educate and inspire. Nelson Mandela used stories to mobilize the anti-apartheid movement, paint a picture of equality, justice, and freedom, and outline his vision for the future of South Africa.

The great communicators cut us with the narratives they created and their dreams for a future and better world. That's what we have to get to. That's the kind of communication we need in these times, and that communication would start with me. It's going to be absolutely vital that I tell a story every time I step in front of an audience. I will tell a story about the story. I'll recount a chapter from a longer story. I'll add verse and material content to the story. I will use stories to remind people who we are, what we're doing, and why it matters. I will use stories to convey the benefit of the work we're doing.

I'll use stories to reveal when we are off track and reinforce when we're on track. I will use stories to measure our progress and to announce when we have arrived. Stories that will help us understand when we need to course-correct or admit that things aren't working quite how we hoped they would.

We must tell stories. Better stories. Consistent stories. Unrelenting stories.

Storytelling Tools

Tools can help us. We need to be as comfortable and knowledgeable about those tools and as fluent as the other powers that are leveraging them to tell their stories.

You know, the metaverse will be here soon. It's a virtual world that allows people to be in the same place even when they are continents apart. Picture that scene from the film, *The Kingsman: The Golden Circle*, when the Kingsman headquarters is destroyed, and the surviving agents use virtual communication to meet. Wearing special glasses, they could see avatar constructs of their fellow agents, who in reality are scattered across the world. By leveraging technology, the agents can discuss their situation, plan a response to the threat they face, and coordinate their efforts to save the world.

Why couldn't the president do something like that? Why couldn't we give a thousand people, a hundred thousand people, a million people devices that would allow us to have a fireside chat? I could virtually appear right in their homes with them. Along a similar vein, why couldn't we set up our own social media? Why not create a device that immediately signals an inaccurate statement or assumption? We are building tools to carry us to Mars. We built the James Webb Telescope. We're building self-driving cars and self flying planes. Certainly, we can develop cutting-edge communication tools. Our government is capable of designing extraordinary technology. I think technology needs to be turned inward to help us govern better and more equitably.

The government needs more speed and clarity. We don't have all day. The clock is ticking, and these issues are worsened by our inactivity and our inability to execute. Let's get something done. I love rolling up my sleeves and getting my hands dirty.

At the risk of sounding conceited, when I step back and I look at what I've accomplished, it's impressive. My former employers will tell you that when they hired me, I told them I would exceed their expectations. And in every case, I did.

I remember in 2007, Steve Jobs strode onto a stage and held up a phone. I recall thinking, "We don't need another phone. We've got Nokia. We have Sony. We've got Motorola. We have got BlackBerry. We even had flip phones like Star Trek tricorders. Do we really need another phone?"

Guess what? We needed another phone.

We didn't know it, but we needed the iPhone. It changed our lives in more ways than we could have imagined at the time. We needed a phone that entertained us, educated us, and better connected us to one another. We needed a phone that located our destinations for us, paid for things we bought, took great photos and warned us of imminent dangers. Within a few years, many of us could not remember a time when we did not have this wonderful communication device in our pocket. When we tried to remember those times, we wondered how we managed to get by. It altered what we do and how we do it.

Now, not all of the change was for the good, but many of the features have become indispensable. And we didn't know we had those needs or expectations until someone showed us and said, "You need this. It will change your life." That is what I mean by exceeding expectations we didn't even know we had.

And that's what my administration will do—over and over again. Exceeding expectations we didn't even know we had. Accomplishing things in unique and novel ways that are repeatable, sustainable, and scalable.

Leaving a Roadmap

Some time ago, early in my career, I would walk into a situation and orchestrate transformational change. However, I would do it in a way that didn't adhere to the scientific process. In other words, others couldn't walk in, learn my process, repeat what I had done, and achieve similar results. You could see the benefits of what had happened. You could see the transformation. But I did not leave a roadmap or a discernible process that was sustainable beyond me. I did not show others how they could do it. I didn't create this kind of intellectual progression.

As president, I will not repeat that practice. We will build models that identify priorities, create value, and bring a measurable return on investment. We'll account for limited resources and diminishing returns. And we'll do it in a way that others can build on. We will create a level of forward momentum at every level of government and every level of the private sector. And this will become a living example. It will become a construct that others can use to create a similar sense of value and achieve similar progress.

Let's talk about foreign policy. Prior administrations have promoted "America first." I would never put America second, but I don't know if we can work with an attitude that we always put America's needs ahead of all our fellow global neighbors. I don't know if we can think that way.

Our impact on the world is far too great to think that we don't have an obligation to be responsible global citizens. We need to be that, and I don't know that we've always been that. I'm not saying that our way of life and culture is always the right way to do things, but we can't deny what we are and how what we do impacts the rest of the world.

The global pandemic illustrated, above everything else, how connected we are on this planet. Yet when we developed cures, we held so much back for ourselves at the expense of the rest of the world, causing the pandemic to last far longer than it should have and causing far more damage than it should have because we didn't think of ourselves as part of a global solution.

We must understand that there's only one planet. We don't have a plan B. We don't have a Planet B. There's only one planet, and our role on this earth is outsized by the good fortune we've had and the responsibility that comes with that good fortune.

This is where the chess games in Washington Square Park are an appropriate analogy. We could make a million moves, but there are only ten things we should do. Figuring out those ten things is crucial to executing and winning the game. We must be kings at execution, and my administration will be just that. We are going to be masters of execution, and we're going to be masters at figuring out what matters most to execute and doing it in a manner that drives lasting and sustainable value.

The Role of Technology

This is also where technology once again comes into play. There is much to be concerned about in the management and application of artificial intelligence. Any reasonable person has to wonder if we have the wisdom to be trusted with the potential power AI wields. However, with the dangers also come great possibilities, so it's imperative that we become absolutely fluent in and competent with it. And we have to begin to utilize it in novel ways that aren't left to the private sector to figure out. We must find ways to use it to help solve some of these really thorny issues that we haven't been able to get our arms around yet.

It's time to execute change. I can't wait for that. That's where the fun begins. We've been practicing. We've been working out, and we've got our bodies right. We've got the speed. We've got the endurance. We've been talking about it, watching films, and visualizing our success. Now it's time to play. Warm-ups are over. It's time to get busy and execute our game plan. I can't wait to get in the arena, get busy, and start making a difference.

Remember that story about Michael Bloomberg setting up his office in the middle of the activity, in the "bullpen?" We are going to mimic that hive methodology. We will not be sitting in the White House, watching the proceedings from afar. No, we'll be right there on Capitol Hill, working with Congress to get things done—not as an adversary, but as a comrade, a colleague, and a co-creator. We may all have different views of what the priorities should be or how to address those priorities. But we will work together with good intentions because we all want the best for this country.

It's just a matter of how we get there. It's a matter of demanding every single day that we get there and that we do the work, however difficult it may be. And we don't settle for anything less than getting there. We owe it to ourselves, our constituents, our children, and the world. The time for anything else is over.

A key question is how to involve the public in this process. Right now, politicians rely on polls to gauge the sentiment of their constituency. I think you have to be careful with polls. It's difficult to get a representative sample. Moreover, polls are unreliable. People will say one thing in polls and then vote the opposite at election time. Polls would tell you that most Americans want some form of gun control, for example. Yet candidates who run under the guise of gun control often lose their election, and those who suddenly take on the mantle of gun control once they're in office are often voted out of office. This belies the results of the polls. There's a difference between what people say and what they do or truly want. Trying to discern that is the tricky part. That doesn't mean you don't ask. It doesn't mean that you don't take note. It doesn't mean you don't want people to be part of the discourse.

A better approach is to talk directly to the people. I know the president has a job to do and needs to be in the office, but I think the job demands more direct interaction with the public.

There are lots of ways you can do that. Why couldn't you have a national Zoom call? Once a week, twice a week, Saturday morning, where you're just talking to people. Why couldn't the president have a rolling list of 100 people who would join him on a Zoom call? Participants could be randomly chosen, and you would select a representative sample. We would want different religions and people from different backgrounds. Why couldn't we do that?

There are creative ways to get the public engaged and involved—things we may not have even thought of yet. It would be valuable to hear directly from the horse's mouth what's going on and know that it's an opportunity for transparency, exposure, and interaction. There is nothing standing between the presidency and the people. We can make that happen.

We need to have a diverse array of voices sitting at the table. For example, I am in favor of gun regulation, but I'd nevertheless love to have the National Rifle Association at the table when we discuss what that looks like. The only criterion is that they are logical, rational people. I want to have the broadest view of what's rational, and the opportunity to have them at the table and part of the solution would be productive and welcomed.

We also want the smartest, most innovative people at the table. The innovations that we bring into the world through organizations like the Defense Advanced Research Projects Agency are absolutely mind-bending. Really smart people are out there, and most of them don't work for the government. Some don't want anything to do with the government, but imagine what organizations like Microsoft, Google, and Meta can bring to the table. These people, if given the opportunity to be part of the solution without all the BS and nonsense associated with it, would gladly work with us; in some cases, they already do. We can bring the best and brightest to the table.

The value of diverse voices, at this point, has been well-established. It's crazy to think that some "solutions" are still produced without a diversity of voices. For example, Kohler, the appliance maker, came out with a faucet that turns on automatically when you put your hand under it. Great innovation. The problem was that they had a dearth of people of color in the room as they were discussing this innovation. When a person of color puts their hand under the faucet, it didn't work because the device does not recognize the pigmentation in their skin. It is unbelievable that no one in that room thought, "Hey, I wonder what happens if a Black person tries to use this?" That's what happens when you don't have diverse points of view; you wind up with something that, when you implement it, is laughably limited.

I would keep this in mind as we source seats at the table. It must be done in an equitable way that takes advantage of the extraordinary diversity we have in this country. Our diversity is our secret sauce.

Chapter 6

The First Task as President

Legendary UCLA basketball coach John Wooden often told his players to "be quick, but don't hurry." It was one of the guiding principles Wooden tried to instill in his players, who included the great Kareem Abdul-Jabbar, Bill Walton, Jamaal Wilkes, and many others. The phrase embraced this idea of combining speed with poise. To win, Wooden suggested, you must be prepared to respond quickly and make decisions without unnecessary delay. At the same time, you need to maintain control and composure and avoid poor decisions in a fast-paced situation.

This will be a guiding principle of my presidential administration. From the outset, we will respond quickly and decisively, yet in an agile and coordinated fashion. It goes back to the high-speed chess in Washington Square Park. As the country's leader, I need to sort through the thousands of possible moves I *could* make to focus on the ten moves I *must* make. When you choose the right ten things and execute them, you go on to affect thousands of things.

Building a Team

One of the first and most critical areas I'll focus on is building my team. We must have a high-performing team. Over the last twenty or more years, we have had a dearth of talent in government, and I will find a way to reverse that. We want the best and the brightest working in our government. I understand that the best and the brightest often aren't always interested in civic duty, so it will be incumbent upon me to change that perception and build a high-performing team representing different constituencies. We want the best, irrespective of their party. Just as Abraham Lincoln pulled together his "team of rivals"—a concept explored by historian Doris Kearns Goodwin in her book *Team of Rivals: The Political Genius of Abraham Lincoln*—I want the best people, and a diverse slate created without regard to their political allegiances. Lincoln appointed some of his biggest critics and then won them over and enlisted their help through some of the darkest days of our country's history.

Likewise, it is incumbent upon me to find common ground and get to a place where we can actually work together on common interests and common ways to achieve common objectives. It's equally important that we bring together a plethora of ideas and perspectives that reflect who we are and what this country is. These are crucial first steps—define a vision, establish a mission, build a common sense of purpose, and design a shared mental model of what success looks like.

Areas of Focus

Some of the areas that I want to focus on include truth, science, and technology. I call it TST. These three elements must be woven through everything we do.

We'll start with the truth because, as Jesus noted in the Gospel of John in the New Testament, "Then you will know the truth, and the truth will set you free." And we must get to the truth.

This doesn't mean I'm going to be some kind of morality cop. It doesn't mean that I and others in the administration won't make mistakes. It doesn't mean we are shedding our humanity and rising above all—how we think, act, and represent truth. However, it's crucial that we all understand truth, understand what truth is and what that means. And the closer we can get to the facts and the reality, the more capable we're going to be to address these issues in fundamental ways that benefit everyone.

Using science, meanwhile, doesn't mean that I'm going to forego my faith or my beliefs. It doesn't mean that there aren't things that science can't explain. But truth, science, and facts kind of all go together.

We want to be able to measure things. We want to be able to understand things. We want things to be grounded in some type of reality that, again, allows us to explain it, understand it, measure it, manipulate it, control it, scale it, and repeat it. Science is a critical component.

Leveraging Technology

For a country as technologically advanced as we are, our government is far behind in the tools we use, how we lean into and leverage technology, and even our ability to interact with some of our tech giants. Many people in government don't even understand technology, even though technology is ubiquitous and part of every phase of our lives.

However, in my administration, we'll strive to leverage technology to drive solutions and create outcomes that will push us further along as a country.

For instance, technology will help us manage how guns are handled and how they can be matched to owners in ways that would prevent others from acquiring and using them for purposes beyond the intentions of the original owner. That technology exists and using it would give us a chance to have different outcomes than the violence we have endured and see on a daily basis.

Listening to the People

Secondly, we need to spend some time listening. I wouldn't be the first president to do this—others have taken train rides across the country, for example, and made whistle stops to meet the crowds and share ideas. But I think it's going to be super important to spend some time listening to a plethora of people—not just to the people who voted for me or who like me, and not just in places that have supported me—but to everyone. I want to give folks an opportunity to have some say about what they think are the issues, the challenges, and the potential solutions.

I want to spend thirty days or so listening. Remember, we've got to be quick, but we're not going to hurry. I remember an exercise I did at a corporate retreat. We were with people we worked with and knew well, and we were divided into groups. Each person was asked to sit quietly while the rest of the group gave them feedback. The individual could not speak, challenge, or respond—just listen. You would be surprised at how difficult that is, to sit there and listen to other people talk about you. But it's a really fascinating kind of exercise to actively listen. That's what I want to do with citizens across the country.

This is not going to go on endlessly. We are not going to be paralyzed by analysis. But we are going to spend a significant amount of time listening.

Building Unity

From there, we can formulate ideas centered on this notion that there are ten things that we're going to focus on and execute right out of the box. What will give us the biggest return on our investment? Which ten things will have an exponential impact? And to the extent possible, I don't want to respond with executive orders. I don't want to rule by fiat. We need consensus and no doubt there will be some compromises. There will be things that must get done and some things from previous administrations that will need to be undone. And I will lead that effort from the Hill, from our version of Bloomberg's bullpen.

I will spend a lot of time in the fray. I understand there are three separate branches of government that are intended to work independently, but at the end of the day, the presidency and Congress have to work together—be it me on the Hill with lawmakers or lawmakers coming to the White House. Brew the coffee. Roll up the sleeves. Get to work.

I think it's important for me to be on their turf, in their space, and for us to be seen working together, arguing and throwing shoes at one another. Whatever it takes.

I love those scenes in the British Parliament with the Prime Minister, when everyone is screaming, and it appears to be total chaos. But I think there's some merit to that messy display. It shows passion. It reveals the urgency all parties feel. As president, I want to be in the fray. I don't want to be above the fray. I admire Barack Obama, but too often his exhortation to Congress to "send me a bill" came across, to me, as too passive.

I know my chief of staff and political advisers will be working and negotiating, and they will continue to do that. But I want to be in the mix, mixing it up. In the Broadway musical *Hamilton*, in the song "The Room Where It Happens," Aaron Burr wants to be present when Alexander Hamilton, Thomas Jefferson, and James Madison reach a compromise to move the United States' capital to Washington, D.C. Burr says, "I want to be in the room where it happens," and the phrase reflects Burr's desire to be part of important decisions that shape history.

I want to go from office to office, knocking on doors and asking, "What's going on? What are you thinking? What's it going to take? How are we going to get this done? What matters to you? What's holding you back? What can help you? How can I help you?" This is how we can get things done. Hand-to-hand combat. Door-to-door combat. Face-to-face discussions. I don't see any reason why that can't be done. I think the gravity of our situation—the enormity of the problems, the enormity of the challenges, the opportunities that are out there, the challenges if we don't move forward—is such that we can't do what we've always done and expect a different set of outcomes. That would be insanity, indeed.

Every president has talked about bipartisanship and going across the aisle. But we continue to maintain traditions that don't encourage collaboration and bipartisanship. It's time to do something different. It's time to do something adventurous. If this book accomplishes anything, I hope it shows how I'm capable of preposterously audacious things.

Developing a bullpen and listening to the people is how we'll build unity and consensus. I don't want an administration of little me's running around. I don't want an administration of people who simply see the world as I see it. Our goal is to get something done. We are here to execute. We are here to win. Moreover, we're committed to getting things done by any means necessary within the rules we operate under. The ideas will come from every corner. In hockey, for example, it's not necessarily the pass to the player who makes the goal that is celebrated and rewarded. It's the pass to the player who makes the pass to the person who scores the goal that is also recognized and rewarded. We want to build that kind of muscle memory, that kind of capability. No idea is a bad idea, and we're constantly challenging ourselves to be better, do better, and get things done.

Using technology, I want to have a 24/7 administration. I want to accomplish in four years what other administrations have needed eight years or more to accomplish. We are going to be relentless. We have to be. If things like the climate clock are spot on, we don't have much time to make these changes and get this work done.

The Point Guard President

It's going to take great communication. That's a core competency of mine, so we'll communicate effectively daily. We will own the message—not just in terms of what I say but in terms of what people hear. As a leader and someone who wants to get things done, I constantly challenge myself to communicate so that people listen. They hear me. I'm inspiring them to act.

I want my whole administration to think this way. To bridge that divide, you need authentic empathy. People need to feel heard. They need to know you are cognizant of what matters to them.

The whole idea of mixing with my fellow lawmakers and government officials represents an enormous opportunity to think differently about how our government works, how we can make positive change, and how we can move things forward. It takes away the us-against-them mentality. It's *all* about us. It's about each of us being present, responsible, accountable, inspired, relevant, and interested in making change, regardless of who gets the credit. Harry Truman, our thirty-third president, is credited with once saying, "It's amazing what you can get accomplished when you don't care who gets the credit." There is no definitive evidence that Truman used these exact words, but it certainly fits his leadership style and beliefs. He often emphasized focusing on the task at hand rather than on personal recognition. I love the quote because it highlights the importance of teamwork, collaboration, and munificence.

As a point guard in basketball, part of my job was to make the game easier for everyone else. When others found it easy to be the best they could be, we won. My job was to orchestrate and manage their game on their behalf. Point guards may not accumulate a lot of points, rebounds, or even assists, but the advanced analytics reveal that when a good point guard is on the floor, good things happen.

When I'm on the floor, things flow. The ball moves. People get open. People cut harder because they know if they move, they'll get the ball. They'll get their opportunity. They understand if they play their role—they set their screen, move without the ball, go after that rebound, and hustle—good things happen. Good things happen for them, and good things happen for the team.

So, as president, I'll play the point guard position. I'll foster that kind of successful environment. That's my mindset, and that's the mindset that will proliferate throughout my administration and the team that we build.

Building that team from the start, focusing on truth, science, and tech. Listening in an active, empathetic way. Being quick but not hurrying. Understanding the ten things that we're going to do that are going to impact and change a thousand things. Getting into the mix, being in the room, going door to door. Creating that sense of ownership, responsibility, and shared mental model of success. These are all the first tasks I'll tackle as we build a common sense of purpose throughout my administration and throughout all levels of government. We'll hold ourselves accountable and responsible.

As a point guard, I'll create those opportunities for others to thrive, gain recognition, and fulfill agendas that fold into what's best for the country, our people, and the world.

That's how I see those early days of the administration unfolding.

Universal Truths

How do we ensure we are speaking a truth that is universally true? That comes from the shared mental knowledge, effective communication, and periodic reassessment to ensure this represents the truth as we know it. Today's truth may not be tomorrow's truth, so we must continually reaffirm it and agree collectively on what represents our truth. We don't assume the truth we hold is the same truth we had a month ago or six months ago. We check ourselves. We agree to hold ourselves accountable to this truth and these methods to achieve our shared goals. When we stray, we course-correct.

In banking, we used this methodology called Agile, and we were relentlessly committed to this practice. We built a curriculum around it to train the auditors and risk people on the practice. It helped them to understand our lexicon and the software development culture. They understood why we were doing what we did, how it was going, and what we hoped to achieve. Some jumped in immediately while others had to be dragged in, kicking and screaming. Eventually, we got everyone moving to the deep end of the pool, swimming freely. Sometimes, we would fall back into our old habits or create new habits that didn't align with the methodology, so we would circle back and reaffirm the right practices and make sure everyone was aligned. Over time, those realignments became less frequent. It became our truth. It's not one person's truth forced on others. It wasn't a Democratic truth or a Republican truth. It's our shared truth because we're all sitting at the table, looking at the same thing. And we do not get up from the table until we've come to a collective agreement.

This is the process we'll use in the White House. We'll continue to march. We'll continue to go towards the light, towards optimism.

I understand that some people may be skeptical. They will say, "We've tried this before," or "That won't work here. We don't do things that way." Even people who support me will question this approach. They will say it sounds too far-fetched, too squishy. But these people never saw me coming.

Let me explain.

Years and years ago, my grandfather in Pittsburgh founded a church and had services in his home. My grandfather was a builder by trade and a steelworker at U.S. Steel, but the church was his passion. When the congregation got too big, he bought a house down the street for the church. When that place got too small, my grandfather went to a Port Authority building nearby that the city was demolishing, and he stopped and talked to the foreman overseeing the takedown.

"How much for all these bricks?" my grandfather asked.

The foreman looked at him skeptically. My grandfather was unkempt and wearing old clothes.

"Old man," he said. "Why are you bothering me?"

"I'd like to buy these bricks."

"For what?"

"Well, I have a church."

An even deeper look of skepticism.

"You got a church?" the foreman said. "All right. I'll sell you these bricks." And so, he charged my grandfather an arm and a leg for the bricks. I'm not even sure the bricks were his to sell.

Months later, they held an opening ceremony for the new church, built with the bricks from the Port Authority building. I was there that day when the foreman showed up. Of course, he recognized my grandfather, and then he recognized the bricks. A smile broke across his face.

"I had no idea who you were," the foreman said. A few days later, he returned all the money my grandfather had paid him for the bricks.

That man never saw my grandfather coming. I remember that day, and when I went on to play basketball at Boston University, that was my philosophy: Never let them see you coming. I was a five-foot-ten-inch point guard playing a tall person's game, and my opponents never saw me coming. By the time they did, it was too late.

So, I expect the naysayers to be out in force. And they'll have good reasons for being naysayers. They will doubt every aspect and every step that we're going to take. But, in the end, they won't see me coming.

Chapter 7

Facilitating a Coalition of the Willing

Several years ago, at a senior management leadership offsite, the participants were given a personality evaluation. The exercise aimed to help us better understand our respective personality characteristics and share that information with our colleagues so that we could function more effectively as a leadership team. After responding to questions probing dimensions like assertiveness, sociability, and intelligence, I discovered my spirit animal: the owl. This revelation was both surprising and enlightening.

The owl, celebrated for its unparalleled vision and majestic ability to navigate the skies, resonates deeply with my journey. There is a profound duality in how the owl reigns over the expanse of the heavens yet can dive with precision toward its goal. It can soar to great heights and swoop down at incredible speeds to get what they want at any given time. That dichotomy—of ascending to great heights before hurtling to the earth at extraordinary speed—made sense to me. It embodies the internal balance of forces I often experience, the yin and yang that coexist within my life and leadership style.

This duality is consistently reflected in my approach to building teams—groups unified by a common purpose and a shared collective understanding of success that serves to lay the groundwork for high performance. When teams and people have a clear sense of purpose and a shared understanding of what constitutes success, you have the core ingredients for success. That's when the fun begins. It is important to note, however, that it's not uniformity in thought or approach that strengthens a team but rather the clarity of the mission and the shared vision of success that amplifies our potential. Disparate opinions and diverse personalities can enrich the process so long as the overarching objectives are crystal clear.

As a leader, it is my responsibility to chart the course and cultivate a shared ambition, securing the commitment and contributions of all team members. The leader sets the vision and creates that sense of purpose concerning the vision, as well as the rationale and criticality for striving toward it, while the team collectively navigates the path to get there. Each person should feel that their voice is heard, and their perspective valued, even if their role is not center stage. This collaborative spirit, where every contribution steers us closer to our goals, truly drives a coalition of the willing.

Creating the Vision

When I launched my second business, the Knowhere Art Gallery on Martha's Vineyard, I began the effort by creating a comprehensive vision and mission statement. Based on my prior experience, having that artifact would be a paramount part of any future success we might secure. I clearly and painstakingly outlined who we were and how we would leverage our platform. Just as importantly, I outlined things that we would not do and directions we would not pursue. Said another way: I knew precisely what we aimed to achieve and what we would deliberately avoid. Since opening, we've been offered countless opportunities to do interesting things. However, if those things don't align with the vision, saying no has been a very straightforward process. This clarity has made it effortless to decline opportunities that do not align with our core objectives. I believe that it was Steve Jobs who said, "Deciding what not to do is as important as deciding what to do."

Today, the gallery's team members don't just work within the vision; they see themselves as integral parts of it. Our success to date has been a testament to our vision-driven focus.

While the vision originated with me, it has become our collective compass, clearly articulating our common purpose, our commitment to the community, and our shared aspirations. This vision-based approach is a philosophy and practice that has served me well across various ventures, both private and professional, and one I plan to carry into the highest office.

Authentic leadership is about charting a course—creating a narrative regarding where we are heading, why the journey matters, and describing the milestones and challenges along the way. It's about articulating a vision compelling enough to set things in motion, then bringing together a cadre of exceptional minds to actualize that vision, and finally, getting out of their way and resisting any urge to micromanage. A leader's task is not to lead the charge in intellect but to facilitate, to dismantle barriers that impede progress, and to empower those smarter voices to elevate the collective vision. Your job is not to be the smartest person on your team. If you are, that's a problem.

As President, it is not my job, nor do I aspire to be the pinnacle of wisdom in the room, but rather the enabler of brilliance. My role will be to clear the path and create and sustain momentum toward our shared destination.

This is why I will be drawn to the halls of Capitol Hill and why the bullpen concept resonates so strongly with me. With so much of communication being nonverbal (70 percent of communication is nonverbal), I believe in the power of presence and the ability to gauge commitment beyond words. People often say things that their body and nonverbal communication clearly indicate they don't mean. Hence, I am vigilant in reading the unsaid, ready to address hesitation, and to call upon the skeptics to voice their concerns so we can forge ahead, united.

I encounter that headshaking yes, body saying no paradigm every day. We all do. Hence, I love looking people in the eye as I'm talking about transformation and change and reading that 70 percent of nonverbal communication that tells me whether they are genuinely bought-in, committed, and focused, or not. And when I see that they have not bought-in, I call them out. "I can see you're not on board," I'll say. "I see you're nodding your head, but I can tell you're not on board. Please share what you're thinking. Allow me to address your issues with what I just described."

In this way, we work through them. That's me, the owl, swooping down from a great height and removing those impediments that prevent us from moving forward. That's why being in the place and in the room where those decisions are made is so important. You're not pulling rank unless you have to. Instead, you are part of the whole process. As a leader, I'm not looking to simply create a coalition of like-minded individuals. I am not seeking a mere echo chamber or a group bound by passive agreement. I don't want a coalition of compromise, nor do I want a coalition of people who all think the same or think like me. I welcome and indeed seek out the dissenting voices and the contrarian perspectives. Once the vision is set and our shared goals are outlined, the tumultuous middle ground becomes fertile soil for progress. It's in this space that the stew of ideas simmers until it's rich with flavor, each ingredient integral to the final masterpiece.

I want dissenting opinions. I want opinions that don't look like mine or function like mine.

As long as we've described the vision, created that sense of purpose, and developed a shared mental model of success, the stuff in the middle—the chaos, discourse, and discomfort of all the things in the middle—becomes essential to the process.

It is like a big pot of stew. Some ingredients don't always look like they go together until they do. And then you can't imagine it being any other way.

I've seen this happen. I've lived it.

Many Voices, One Chorus

In 2008, at a major banking institution, I became the lone champion of Agile, a software development approach that accommodates and embraces change rather than resisting it, resulting in products, services, and applications that evolve over the development life cycle. The end state is significantly more relevant and provides greater value and sustainable utility. Agile doesn't lock out change. The process is malleable and able to absorb changes in real time so that the emerging product keeps pace with advancements in the world. Agile kept us at the cutting edge.

Being the sole advocate for Agile did not win me any popularity contests. When I began leveraging the methodology, I was the only person in a firm of more than 200,000 people using this approach. Colleagues, executives, and even my team members viewed me with extreme skepticism—as an iconoclast shaking the foundations of the established order. I was a heretic. Yet, as time passed and our successes began to overshadow our setbacks, the tide turned.

One of my direct reports, a remarkably astute and brilliant woman, initially stood firmly against the Agile tide. Outwardly compliant and inwardly critical, she dedicated her energy to disproving the methodology I championed. But slowly and surely—as we knocked down barriers, dismantled hurdles, and overcame impediments, and as we began to enjoy success where we once encountered failure—her perspective shifted dramatically. She transitioned from a skeptic to a staunch advocate. After I left the company, she went on to become an evangelist and an organizational guru for Agile. She still recounts the story of how she once fought the approach she now champions. Today, like me, she is called an Agile evangelist.

This evolution wasn't coincidental; it was facilitated by a leadership style that welcomes dissent. Giving her the opportunity to dissent only made her consent more solid, more committed, and more focused. A lot of leaders would have seen her opposition and tried to marginalize her or show her out. I, however, invited her voice into the room, into the conversation. I engaged her critique, providing a platform for her to voice concerns and contribute insights. I said, "Give me the reason why you're dissenting. Show me what you think is wrong. Show me where you think this might go astray." With this approach, she had the agency to point out some very insightful and valuable points about where we might be able to do things better. And we did! This approach helped to win her over and strengthen our work. Her skepticism wasn't shunned but was utilized to refine our practice, earning her genuine buy-in and fostering a deeper commitment to the Agile path.

This is the approach I intend to transplant into the White House: convening a symphony of disparate voices, not seeking echo chambers but embracing discordant notes. It's not about assembling "Ralph thinkers" or Ralph acolytes but about uniting under the banner of progress, acknowledging that substantive change is an imperative whose time is now. By welcoming divergent opinions, we'll forge a consensus that is robust, resilient, and ready to navigate the complexities of governance.

Sudden, Drastic Change

For a decade, Hawai'i has been my refuge from the holiday blues. It has been an antidote for the crushing depression I typically feel around that time of year. Hawai'i is close enough to feel connected yet far enough to offer escape. Every device, every familiar convenience, operates just the same as in the Northeast, providing a seamless transition from mainland life to island serenity.

At first, we thought we would go to different islands, and no doubt, someday, we will. However, we found paradise in Maui, and it has become my holiday sanctuary. There, among its sun-kissed beaches and welcoming storefronts, I've forged friendships that have transcended the annual visits. Yet, as I pen these words, one of the island's idyllic towns, Lahaina, exists only in memory. In one of the worst tragedies to ever strike Maui, Lahaina burned to the ground in late 2023. A fierce wildfire, fueled by climate change's unpredictable wrath, reduced this beloved town to ashes. The fire erupted and spread incredibly quickly, thanks in part to unusually warm temperatures and high winds. The historic banyan tree, a sentinel from the era of Hawaiian royalty, stands as a solitary witness to what was and what's been lost.

Such is the nature of change—swift and unyielding. It's a stark reminder that our status quo is not just unsustainable; it's perilous. The present path we tread, as custodians of the earth, demands a pivot. The course that we are on as a nation is not something that we can or should maintain. Moreover, the window for change—the window to affect the kind of change that alters some of these inevitable outcomes if we stay on the path we're on—is closing. It is closing by the day. The opportunity to affect change that will benefit us, that will save us, is slipping through our fingers.

The coalition we assemble will be grounded in this reality. The debates on the nature of our evolution will be fervent but welcome. Discourse is the crucible in which better strategies will be forged. As we confront the unexpected and collectively reshape our thinking, it is my intent to ensure that the clamor and friction will serve us well.

To say the discussions will be spirited would be an understatement. Some time ago, I saw a quote from Randy Pausch in a Jimmy John's restaurant that said, "Honesty is not only morally right, but it is also highly efficient." There will undoubtedly be yelling and screaming. I imagine there is going to be cursing, which will be interesting coming from the grandson of a devout Pentecostal minister. (And science tells us profanity in the workplace is actually good, which works for me.) However, the swearing, sweating, and conflict will be to our advantage. What comes out of this cacophony, this tempest of opinions and emotions, will be a stronger union of this coalition and will forge a more resilient collective.

Everyone Has Good Intentions

When people understand and believe that their voices and opinions are respected and valued, they are more likely to participate in creating and carrying out solutions. People stand behind initiatives they have a hand in shaping, and they support what they help create; it's as simple as that.

We will operate under essential ground rules in the White House: assume good intentions in every idea presented and give everyone the benefit of the doubt, fostering an atmosphere where honorable intentions are the norm. We're going to make the White House a safe place to disagree. It will be a sanctuary for constructive disagreement, where persistent discourse is encouraged until breakthroughs are achieved. We can have all the battles we want, and we'll stay at it until we find that epiphany. If you don't agree, you need to say it. Silence is not an option; dissent must be voiced. Because when we walk out that door, we walk out united. We walk out as a force. Once we leave here, it's all about execution. When we stand up from the table, the discourse ends, and execution—with all the commitment and alignment we can muster—will begin. After our discussions, unity will be our hallmark, with a commitment to action that is as strong as the fervor of our dialogue.

Where people find themselves in trouble with me is when they are not honest and authentic about what they think. That's why authenticity is our watchword. If you're not on board, say you're not on board. You cannot pretend to back something that you disagree with, having never voiced your dissent. Disguised agreement is the antithesis of the trust and integrity we stand for. So, everyone must talk about why they're not on board. They must give us the opportunity to address whatever is getting in the way of their support. They must openly express reservations and allow us the chance to navigate and resolve them. That is how trust is forged and maintained.

Our collective dedication to positive ideation, change, and exhaustive execution must mirror the resolve of marathon runners, whose commitment is unfeigned and exhaustive.

You cannot fake a marathon. You cannot fake running twenty-six miles. If you are not committed to and passionate about marathons, you're not going to be able to do it.

That fifth mile, tenth mile, twelfth mile, and twentieth mile... each one brings its own intimidating weight. You reach a point when your body is screaming. "Stop. I can't do it—won't do it. I'm going to quit." That's your mind talking, and if you're going to finish, you have to ignore it. Your will, courage, and determination are what carry you through to the finish.

In 2019, Marine Corps veteran Micah Herndon ran for some of his fallen comrades who were lost during their tour of duty in Afghanistan. Towards the end of the race, Herndon's body broke down, and he dropped to the ground. He was unable to rise to his feet and stand. Running was out of the question. People ran to his side to help, but he angrily waved them away. "Stop!" he yelled. "Get away. I'm finishing." And he did. He literally crawled across the finish line on his hands and knees. What an amazing act and example of courage and commitment.

That is the very definition of commitment. You can't fake that. You can't disguise that. If you don't have it, you simply don't have it.

Our four years in the White House are going to be like that marathon. Just as every mile of a marathon tests the runner's resolve, our journey will challenge our collective will, courage, commitment, and endurance. It is going to be 24/7. You won't hear me talking about vacationing. You won't see me taking time off. You won't hear me talking about time away. Our tenure will be relentless, marked not by leisure but by urgency. We are both in a marathon and a race against time. It's a race against looming events, the likes of which this planet has never seen. And we must and will work with a ceaseless sense of urgency and purpose.

And if someone is not passionate about the work that we're doing, they will not be able to fool this coalition. You *may* mislead this coalition for a little while in terms of your commitment, faith, and passion for the work that we're doing and the change that we are going to implement. But there will be no room for pretense; passion cannot be feigned in the long run. Ultimately, our coalition will see through any facade of commitment, as our mission is simply too critical to allow for anything less than absolute dedication.

Let me be clear: I am seeking the resolutely committed. You don't have to agree with everything we do, and it's unlikely that every idea someone shares will be adopted. I'm not expecting blind loyalty like some of our recent presidents have demanded. I welcome dissent, but at the end of the day, I expect complete commitment to and support for the work our coalition chooses to do. You'll get your chance to disagree, but in the end, we'll all be loyal to the team and to the true path we map together. United, we will pursue our North Star, dedicating ourselves to a cause that transcends individual interests and serves the greater good.

The Velocity of Change

Change is a relentless tide. Within its currents lie the seeds of growth, strength, and an enhanced alignment with our deepest passions. Rob Siltanen is credited with saying, "The people crazy enough to think they can change the world are the ones that do." Steve Jobs, who often referenced that quote, called these individuals "the misfits, the rebels, and the troublemakers." He said, "You can quote them, disagree with them, glorify or vilify them. However, the only thing you can't do is ignore them. Because they change things, they push the human race forward." You can call it "crazy," or courage, or something else. I am completely convinced that it is this belief, in our willingness to be agents of change, that will enable us to find the path to true progress.

Joining this coalition will demand more than just the stamina to endure; it will also require the passion to prevail. It's about possessing the tenacity to push beyond mile twenty, to tap into that wellspring of determination, and, if need be, to crawl across the finish line in pursuit of our goals.

This fervor and dedication have been the hallmark of my corporate and entrepreneurial endeavors, philanthropic engagements, and personal philosophy, and they've been a part of every team I've led. It's a synergy of selflessness, a collective vision, and a dynamic drive for success. This is the force that will propel us, and WE will tap into it to transform the world.

People will be skeptical. Skepticism often greets transformational change, especially when it arrives unbidden. When I walk into situations, I bring transformational change, even when people don't think they need transformation. If you're not continuously evolving and you're not changing yourself and the world around you in a transformational manner, then you are probably falling behind. As Coach Pitino often said, "If it ain't broke, break it."

There is no treading water. You can't tread water in rip currents! If all you do is tread water, you're going to be pulled and dragged whether you like it or not.

Stagnation is not an option in a world where the currents of innovation constantly shift beneath us. As a licensed scuba diver, I experienced this firsthand during a drift dive in the Caribbean. The boat let us off at one spot, and the captain said, "I'll meet you a mile or two away at another spot." I was thinking that all we were doing was going straight down and looking at the beautiful reefs, fish, and marine life. There was no plan to swim a mile or two, and when we dove, we had no sense that we were moving beyond where our fins propelled us.

Sure enough, we surfaced, and we were nowhere near where we started. The current had taken us two miles away without us even being aware that we were in a current. This invisible force is a metaphor for life's unnoticed yet incessant change.

That's what life is about. That's what this world is about. You may not think that things around you are changing, but they are changing at the speed of light, and the velocity and importance of that change are in view every day. In fact, the velocity is increasing.

Ray Kurzweil, a futurist and inventor, talks about the accelerating pace of technological change. He developed the Law of Accelerating Returns, which declares that technological progress is not linear but exponential. His foresight into the exponential growth of technology reminds us that change compounds at an astonishing rate, bringing together disparate advancements in a synergistic explosion of progress. As technology advances, the rate of change increases, and innovation accelerates. That acceleration is the key to understanding how different technologies—such as AI, biotech, and nanotechnology—will converge in an irreversible fashion. This convergence promises a future that is dense with transformation—what once took a millennium might now unfold in just a century or less.

That's the intense velocity I'm talking about. We don't feel it or see it, but it's happening every day. Regardless of whether you want transformational change, that kind of change is happening. In this maelstrom of progress, resistance is not only futile but counterproductive. I see my role as a guide, helping to steer perceptions about change to illuminate the possibilities that lie beyond the comfort of the familiar. Moving your cheese is not going to be the end of the world. And the place we move your cheese to, you might actually like it better. You might get more cheese. You might get better cheese. Steve Jobs moved cheese and, in doing so, defined new territories of innovation. The iPad, which initially met with intense skepticism, exemplifies the kind of progress that questions the status quo and ventures boldly into the unknown. Today, iPads rank behind iPhones in total sales but ahead of other Apple products like the MacBook, and they're a leading product in the tablet market, valued for its versatility, portability, and performance.

You're going to come out the other side of this change better than when you were just treading water. You're going to know more. You're going to be more capable. You're going to be stronger. You're going to have better skills. You're going to be more in tune with your passions. In any way that you define better, you're going to be better.

Change is indeed an unrelenting tide. However, within its currents and wake lie the means to grow, strengthen, and enhance our alignment with our deepest passions.

Transformational Experience Counts

I am confident in my ability to introduce change, and my track record in leading change initiatives has demonstrated that I can do so successfully. The experience has honed a skill that I find essential: making people comfortable with change. I know how to uncover the WIIFM—which stands for "what's in it for me"— for each individual. I can convince people that change is in their best interest. What's in it for you? Let me help you visualize that. This is what it means; this is how you will benefit. Giving people their WIIFM brings them on board and helps them become the architects of their destiny, the authors of their own stories. It helps them see that story as glorious and fantastic—one they are proud of and comfortable with as we move forward.

Building coalitions is familiar terrain for me, albeit on a smaller scale than the presidency requires. Yet, the essence of the role remains the same: it's about uniting diverse voices towards a shared goal. No candidate truly has presidential experience until they are in the role, save for the incumbent seeking re-election. Every president since George Washington has learned on the job, and I am prepared to continue that tradition.

My professional and philanthropic endeavors have instilled in me a suite of capabilities that are well-suited to the presidency. There is a palpable consensus across the political spectrum that change is imperative. And while opinions on the nature of that change and the means to achieve it may vary widely, the recognition of its necessity does not.

It's this consensus that excites me—the prospect of leading a coalition rich with varying opinions, backgrounds, and ideas unified in the pursuit of transformative goals. The potential of what such a coalition can achieve is boundless. I am ready to steer us toward the incredible possibilities that await when we combine our collective strengths and insights.

Persuasion vs. Coercion

There is often a fine line between coercion and persuasion. Navigating the delicate balance between these two is complex.

I think of a story from the Bible, Revelation in the New Testament, where Jesus uses the imagery of knocking at the door. The image of him knocking represents his desire to have a personal and intimate relationship with people. He doesn't force entry but rather extends an invitation to have faith in him and accept his spiritual guidance and teachings. The message is that people have the choice to accept or reject his invitation, but Jesus will also be patient and persistent in seeking a connection with others.

I interpret it a little differently. To me, the difference between persuasion and coercion is the knocking. That persistent knocking is an invitation to dissent, an opportunity to say yes or no. To me, the story signifies that saying no isn't the end of the world. People are free to say no. They're free to dissent. They're free to go in a different direction. What I'm asking is that they choose in a very intentional, conscious way. Whatever you decide next is a function of choice, not inactivity or crossing your arms and doing nothing. You have an intentional kind of choice to go or stay, to open or not, to participate or walk away.

To me, the knock is an invitation. Hear me. Listen. Give me a chance. Help me understand. What would it take? Those kinds of questions. The only coercion is compelling people to confront the question and make a choice. It's like when the gun goes off at the start of a running race: you either start moving or you stand there. But one way or the other, the moment demands a conscious choice.

That choice is yours to make, but you must choose. Obviously, I have an opinion about what your choice should be. But that opinion involves an extraordinary level of responsibility on my part to help you understand what it means to join this coalition. Why is there value in it for you? Why should it matter to you? It's my job to answer those questions.

Whatever your answer, I bear some responsibility. If the door remains closed, I must consider my part in that outcome. Was my explanation insufficient? Did I relent too soon or make it too easy to turn away? Was my intent lost in translation, or was the personal benefit I promised not compelling enough?

In the end, the decision is yours, and whatever it may be, it prompts reflection on my approach, sharpening my resolve to be more lucid, more convincing, and more worthy of your trust and collaboration.

Chapter 8

The Power of Conversations

Communication is one of my superpowers. It is a defining skill—not because I've mastered it, but because I recognize its intricacies and am deeply committed to continual improvement in it. I am by no means perfect at communicating, however, I recognize how critical it is, and that factors into my drive to be highly proficient at this fundamental competency. My view is that communication is a flowing process where time, space, context, and nonverbal cues all matter greatly.

For example, how much is communicated nonverbally? Researcher Albert Mehrabian found that in certain examples involving feelings and attitudes, words contribute just 7 percent to the overall message, while your tone of voice accounts for 38 percent and body language contributes a whopping 55 percent. These percentages won't hold true for all conversations, but the research does suggest that nonverbal cues are key in augmenting and supporting verbal communication. Their significance and impact vary according to the context and nature of the conversation. In other words, paying close attention to nonverbal cues, either in one-on-one dialogue or group discussions, is critically important to ensuring that your message is understood as intended.

Leadership demands I own not just my words but how they're interpreted. I must take responsibility not only for what I say but for what was heard. The two aren't always the same. I've observed too many situations where what was heard and what was acted on was something completely different. In the military, the term "fast is slow and slow is fast" describes situations where hasty planning or conversation leads to mistakes, setbacks, or inefficiencies. To do communication right, you must speak clearly, ensure full understanding, and listen carefully to the response. You must reflect on what you heard to ensure you received the message properly. In other words, fast communication is slow because it leads to misunderstanding. Slow communication takes time initially but causes fewer setbacks, making it faster.

I played college basketball for Hall of Fame coach Rick Pitino, who is a phenomenal coach and perhaps one of the greatest of all time. Of course, there are the Lombardis, Popoviches, and Belichicks, but Pitino belongs in the pantheon of great coaches. I worked with Coach Pitino as a grad assistant and had great success. Rick wanted me to continue coaching, but at the time, I found it frustrating. I could pull the team over, tell them things, explain things to them, and then watch them go on the floor and do the exact opposite of what I just said. It was absolutely amazing. I would be very clear about what I said, but what transpired didn't reflect anything that I said at all.

Eventually, it dawned on me that these conversations are a bilateral, two-way street, requiring that I take responsibility not only for what I said but for what the players heard.

As we look at what's transpiring in our country and across the world, it's clear that conversations and communication couldn't be more important than they are right now. More than ever, the world needs authentic conversations—a discourse that forges understanding, solves problems, and is not just an exchange of monologues. When I observe conversations today, I watch people talk around one another. I hear people declare how transparent they are when they are not being transparent at all. They are, at best, being opaque. They are not revealing what's in their heart and their head. They talk about honesty in the context of brutality. *I'm going to be brutally honest.* Honesty doesn't have to be brutal. Honesty should not wound. There's nothing about honesty that needs to be brutal. And yet, that's often how we want to frame honesty.

Our discourse today is not leading us to a place of understanding, inspiration, cooperation, and effective problem-solving. And that's assuming we even talk at all. Most of the time, we don't. We hear what others say, but we don't listen. We don't build on their ideas. We just put forth our own ideas and disregard everyone else's. This is not communication. This is not understanding or ideation.

For me to interact with you, we must communicate.

In the absence of that, we are very solitary figures. We misunderstand, and we are misunderstood. The absence of that communication leads to a lot of misunderstandings, missed opportunities, and challenges. We all must strive to communicate better, remembering that good communication stems from good listening.

I call communication as one of my superpowers because I understand its transformative potential and power. I understand that this mechanism will get us where we need to be.

As a basketball coach, when I took responsibility for what I said as well as for what my players heard, I noticed a fascinating transformation. The players went from acting on their own interpretation of what they heard to a collective that acted as a team. They began understanding their respective roles and responsibilities relative to the objectives we were trying to achieve as a team. They heard me and understood what we were trying to achieve because I took responsibility for ensuring that they listened and comprehended my message. They got there because I made sure that what I said was what they heard. And what they heard was something that they could act upon. By ensuring that they didn't just hear but understood, we became a team in the truest sense.

These are incredibly challenging times. With legal proceedings against former and current national figures, we are navigating an era of unparalleled complexity. This tumult is merely the tip of the iceberg, overshadowing the day-to-day crises like the migrant situation in New York, where solutions are urgently needed but remain elusive without effective communication.

We can't solve issues like these if we don't communicate.

Effective dialogue isn't solely about eloquence; it's equally about the art of listening. My capacity to extract information is only as valuable as my ability to listen to what's conveyed. This was a lesson that took shape early in my life, delivered through the words of my father. "I have the world in a jug and the stopper in my hand," he would say, a phrase that baffled me as a child but now resonates with profound clarity.

"I have the world in a jug and the stopper in my hand." It took me a long time to understand what the hell that meant. But he repeated it incessantly. *I have the world in a jug and the stopper in my hand.*

What he meant was that he had answers. He had lots of answers. He had a whole world of answers in a jug and the stopper in his hand. He had it all figured out but lamented that few people would listen to him or engage with him. Despite all his knowledge and wisdom and all the help he could provide with the things that people were trying to do, no one would engage with him.

He was carrying on about this one day when I was at his home in Pittsburgh. I stopped him.

"You know," I said. "If it really matters to you that people engage with you, if it really matters to you that people listen to you, you might want to talk in a way that *allows* people to hear you. For you, that jug and stopper are like hammers with which you bludgeon people. You bludgeoned people with your truth. You bludgeoned people with your wisdom. You bludgeoned people with your point of view. It's your way or the highway. And the result is you drive people away rather than draw them in.

"That's not particularly inviting in terms of engaging with people or people wanting to engage with you. If you've got all these beautiful answers that they could use to perfect their lives or change their course, who wouldn't want to hear that? The problem is that they won't listen when it's coming at them like a hammer."

That moment with my father was pivotal, not only in guiding him but in cementing my own philosophy. I took my own advice to heart. I told my father that I had my own jug and stopper and had things pretty well figured out myself. That wasn't true, of course. It wasn't true then, and it's not true now. But what is true is that whatever answers I may have and whatever thoughts and insights I've gained can't be imparted to people in a manner that they can't hear or are unwilling to listen.

It must be a bilateral exchange, and when it is, it's beautiful. When people know they're going to be heard and that their opinions are going to be respected, it sets the table for great communication. We're not going to agree on everything. We're not going to take every suggestion. That's okay. We're not going to take all day to figure something out because we don't have all day.

An indication of this is that the members of the Science and Security Board have been deeply worried about the deteriorating state of the world. That is why they set the Doomsday Clock at two minutes to midnight in 2019 and at 100 seconds to midnight in 2022. Last year, they expressed their heightened concern by moving the Clock to 90 seconds to midnight—the closest to global catastrophe it has ever been—in large part because of Russian threats to use nuclear weapons in the war in Ukraine.

That environmental clock that I referenced earlier is also ticking, and we can see some of the remnants and the challenges that are happening across the world as climate change unfolds before our eyes. And these are just a few of the myriad challenges we face. So, we don't have all day. We must act. The sense of urgency I feel is compelling me to stand up and do what I'm doing here and now.

The irony is that the only way to solve these imminent problems is to take the time to listen. We must take time to talk. We must take time to engage. Rushing to solutions or failing to take any action at all, is going to be our undoing.

Harnessing the Superpower of Communications

Communication, one of my proclaimed superpowers, is an ever-evolving discipline for me. Each day, I continuously practice not just concise speaking but active listening, eagerly embracing the dual responsibilities of my words and their reception. I constantly ask, "Do we have that crucial common sense of purpose, that shared mental model of success that I talked about? All of that is part of being an effective communicator and effectively communicating.

I eagerly anticipate that in the discourse ahead to hear diverse perspectives and explore ideas on actionable strategies. It is in this exchange of dialogue that we can begin to construct and execute meaningful plans that translate words into tangible action. True communication is the precursor to progress, and the transformational change this country and the world need.

Thereafter, I am looking forward to aggressively leveraging another of my other superpowers, which is getting things done. I want to take that information and put it into a meaningful strategy that will allow us to execute and begin rapidly moving forward. Effective communication is foundational to getting something done.

In 1976, reggae musician Bob Marley was shot during a home invasion in Jamaica. The attack was politically motivated because there was a great deal of political tension in Jamaica at the time, and Marley was an outspoken voice for peace and unity. Despite gunshot wounds to his arm and chest, Marley appeared two days later in the Smile Jamaica Concert, which had been organized to ease political tensions. Marley believed music and love could heal hatred and systemic racism. Still, people questioned why Marley would choose to perform. "Bad people don't take the day off," Marley replied, "so good people have to work harder."

Bob Marley's resilience after his attack in 1976 serves as a profound reminder: the forces that strive to disrupt and destroy have not and will not rest, so our efforts to build and heal must be even more vigorous. We cannot afford to be idle in our quest for good. When evil is relentless, our pursuit of the greater good must be indefatigable.

We cannot take a day off from pursuing and doing good. The bad guys find it so easy to do bad things, but the good people often struggle to get on the same page. We just talk and talk. We talk at each other and back through each other and around each other. However, we don't often speak in a manner that allows us to hear one another. We don't speak in a way that inspires one another. We don't talk in a way that galvanizes, encourages, and lifts us up so that we get good stuff done—quickly and consistently. As a result, far too often, we find ourselves in echo chambers of mindless rhetoric rather than in arenas of meaningful action.

That, however, is what these conversations can lead to. That's what communicating effectively will do. That's why every day I ask myself, "How can I connect with people? How can I touch people? How can I inspire people?" I'm talking about the people I lead, the people I work with, and the people I work for. How can I inspire them to think bigger, think broader, work better, be better, get things done, and end the bureaucracy and other stuff that gets in the way of moving forward? How can I help? How can I communicate in a way that gets us through all of that?

As president, this will be my focus.

I'm excited about how we can leverage different tools and technology to amplify our message. We will ceaselessly endeavor to keep driving with a nonstop, every-moment-of-every-day mentality. We must get something out there that tells our story, tells the truth, and lets people know where we are, what we're doing, why we're doing it, and how we're doing it. We must let people know what they can do and how they can do it. How is this impacting them? And what is their role?

We live in a golden age of information. We are rich in tools that can disseminate this information. The government has limitless opportunities to tell and own its story.

We are going to be an extraordinary communication machine. However, this isn't merely about talking—it's about connecting, influencing, and motivating every individual to play their part. We'll leverage different avenues, tools, and mechanisms to reach people, touch them, and inform them. We'll engage people, talk to people, and be accessible to people. We will make this work in ways that have never been tried. We need people to understand their responsibility and the role they play so that together, we achieve something more, something better, and something lasting.

Powerful, persuasive communicators have several compelling characteristics. For one, they aren't there just to share the good news. They are there in good times and bad. They must be believable and accountable. They are consistent. They don't change their story without a good explanation. There is a congruity between what they say and what they do. They speak in a language that people understand. They speak with power and conviction in ways that inform, entertain, and inspire. They use examples to clarify. They freely admit to gaps in their own understanding, and they are self-aware enough to understand their own biases. They have that rare combination of confidence and vulnerability; they don't pretend to have all the answers, but they certainly know how to pose the right questions—the questions that compel us to act and contribute.

It's like the way Tiger Woods owns his golf swing or how great communicators own their story. When I joined a global financial management company as the head of technology, reporting to the CEO, one of my first hires was someone to lead our communications practice. I purposely called this person a storyteller because I wanted them to assist me (and my leadership team) in telling compelling and motivating stories about our technology organization and our value proposition to our business partners, clients, and shareholders.

This individual became a cornerstone of our organization, elevating our collective ability to communicate effectively by drawing on examples like John F. Kennedy and Martin Luther King Jr.—paragons of storytelling and masters of using anecdotes, parables, and personal experiences to convey, in the case of King, his advocacy for civil rights. King knew that great stories connect with people on an emotional level and compel them into action.

For example, his famous "I Have a Dream" speech was delivered during the March on Washington for Jobs and Freedom in 1963. In that speech, King described the Emancipation Proclamation as a promissory note that had never been honored for African Americans.

"In a sense, we've come to our nation's capital to cash a check," King said. "When the architects of our republic wrote the magnificent words of the Constitution and the Declaration of Independence, they were signing a promissory note to which every American was to be a full heir. This note was a promise that all men, yes, Black men as well as White men, would be guaranteed the unalienable rights of life, liberty, and the pursuit of happiness."

Clearly, the country had defaulted on that debt. This storytelling technique allowed King to frame the struggle for civil rights as a failed promise, making the injustice more relatable and compelling to his audience. His was like a hook inside you, this story of a broken promise.

Above all the aforementioned attributes, the one I hold paramount is clarity. It is the lens that sharpens all other facets of communication. Without clarity, the integrity of your message weakens, and your truth comes under scrutiny. And within this sphere of clarity, context reigns supreme.

Consider Winston Churchill—his tenacity and clarity were once Britain's beacon during its darkest hours. He was exactly who his country needed at the time. Yet, as times shifted, Churchill's failure to adapt rendered his once-remarkable leadership less pertinent. His example underscores that the true measure of a leader lies in their ability to evolve with and adapt to the ebb and flow of circumstances.

Effective Communication and the Ethical Dilemma of Social Media

Over the years, I've learned a few tricks and techniques to ensure people are hearing me correctly. For instance, I'll sometimes ask people to play it back for me: "What did you just hear me say?" In coaching, of course, you'd see right away if the players heard you correctly just by the way they conducted the ensuing play. If it was supposed to be a pick and roll and the center set the pick but never rolled, you would realize you might need to edify the big man.

In those circumstances, it wasn't unusual for me to immediately call another timeout and go through it again, perhaps in a different way, perhaps asking the center to repeat back what he believed his assignment to be. I do the same kinds of things at work. In the private sector, we measure everything we do, so I can see from those metrics whether people have gotten the message. If they haven't, I go through the messaging again. I'll watch their expressions and their body language, and I'll ask them to play it back. When you take your time to ensure you have been heard and that the other person understands, you save a lot of time in the future because you don't have to say the same thing over and over.

As President, I'll embrace social media to reach citizens directly. It is an indispensable tool in our digital age. And yet, I am conflicted about doing so. My engagement with it is tempered by knowledge and caution, especially considering revelations about how platforms such as Facebook—where I must disclose, I have held the Meta stock since its IPO—can exacerbate societal divides and propagate hate speech. The staggering revelations in *The Chaos Machine* present a chilling account of the manipulation woven into the fabric of social media. My discontinuation of personal Facebook use was a decision grounded in ethical concerns, reflecting my unease with the platform's darker implications.

The Stories We Remember

When I think of the best examples of elected officials or government representatives effectively using narratives, I think of George H.W. Bush during Desert Storm, the military operation led by the U.S. and its allies in response to Iraq's invasion of Kuwait in 1990. Our objective was to liberate Kuwait by conducting a large-scale aerial bombing campaign and a ground offensive to push Iraq out of Kuwait. President Bush used rhetoric and storytelling to help people understand the importance of the situation and why the U.S. needed to be involved. His language spoke to people across the world and brought the world together in a way that we had not seen in some time, possibly since World War II. More than a decade later, his son, George W. Bush, was equally compelling in his public statements following the terrorist attack on the Twin Towers in New York City. I was in New York City that day and watched the second plane fly into the World Trade Center, confirming to those of us watching in horror that this was a purposeful attack on our people and our nation's security. I watched everything unfold, and Bush's response was swift and decisive. Like his father, he built an international coalition while he strengthened our defenses at home, creating the Department of Homeland Security and the Transportation Security Administration.

Barack Obama was a galvanizing speaker. His address after the shooting of Black worshippers in South Carolina was comforting but also invigorating. The stories he told and the way he communicated compelled us to address the question of gun responsibility. He didn't let a horrific tragedy go to waste in terms of moving the conversation forward regarding a new paradigm around gun responsibility.

We can't talk about the power of forceful rhetoric without talking about John F. Kennedy's speech announcing the country's plan to put a man on the moon within a decade. At the time, people were stunned by the idea. Talk about a big, hairy, audacious goal—this was certainly one of those. His words sowed the kind of action that snowballed into this movement that pointed us exactly where he said we would be in exactly the timeframes he set. That shows you the power of words. That shows you the value of precise language and urgency.

When you think of these historic moments, you realize that anyone wanting to be president has some very large shoes to fill. However, being president is not always about uniting the nation in times of crisis. Sometimes, it's more about uniting the people sitting around the table and getting them to simply *talk* to one another and build off each other's ideas.

That challenge also requires precision and urgency. Let me share an example of how I managed a situation like that.

It was during my time at a large international banking organization where I managed the technology side of things. We had a large budget, but the department I inherited was misaligned. People did a lot of work and spent gobs of money but had very little to show for it. Our partners elsewhere in the company liked us as people, but they were a little frustrated because we spent a lot, used jargon they didn't understand, and took forever to accomplish anything. And the things that we produced weren't that great. Consequently, we were not high on anyone's Christmas card list.

The Art of Turning 'Impossible' Into 'Achievable'

So, I got a room full of people together. I assembled my developers, project managers, scrum masters, and infrastructure and network team members. They filed in with quizzical expressions. They had no idea what we were doing.

I didn't keep them waiting.

"We're cutting our budget by $10 million."

The room's energy shifted palpably as surprise morphed into concern. Disbelief rippled through the air. Voices of dissent and apprehension rose in chorus, each one echoing the sentiment: "Impossible."

"We're not leaving this room until we cut the budget by $10 million," I continued, utilizing the twin impact of clarity and urgency.

"That's impossible," one person said.

"Yeah, there's a whole bunch of things we want to do," said another.

"What's more," I went on. "After we cut the budget, we're going to significantly ramp up the value and the impact of the work we do and the deliveries we make."

Objections continued, but then I broke in.

"Look, you're telling me this is impossible. However, if we don't do this, I will certainly be fired. But before I get fired, I will make sure I fire all of you. So, let's start saving $10 million."

Suddenly, the art of the impossible became absolutely possible. Like the group I described in an earlier chapter that figured out how to stop power lines from snapping in Canada, this group began creative brainstorming. We looked at how many desk phones our team used and realized we were paying for more than we needed. Boom. We canceled them and saved money. Does everyone need a laptop? No. Half weren't even using them. Boom. More savings. How many desks could we get rid of? How many print jobs were wasting paper? In very little time, we had identified nearly $15 million in savings. Every preposterous idea led to a perfectly reasonable one.

You see, I understood the value of turning the impossible into possible. I grew up under challenging conditions. We had a little money, and there were six of us living in a 960-square-foot house with four rooms. But we flourished. I went on to graduate from a private university and work on Wall Street. I am the living embodiment of what it is to be absolutely delusional and preposterous. From cramped living quarters to a private university degree and a career on Wall Street, I've lived the narrative of the audacious dreamer. This was not unfamiliar territory for me. My name is Ralph H Groce III, but my nickname in the family was simply Third. I recall my cousin's words, a mix of disbelief and awe, acknowledging my unyielding pursuit of dreams once perceived as folly, "Third, man. We all thought you were crazy, completely out of your mind. You'd talk about going to college, playing basketball, living in New York. And you know what? Everything you said, you've done."

So, you see, I've always had a different frame of mind. I live in a world where boundaries and guardrails don't exist—at least not in the places where people think they are. My ethos has been shaped by this perspective: constraints are often illusions. Throughout my life, I've noticed that people are far too willing to embrace the restrictive guardrails and guidelines established by others. And when they meet me and get to know me, they get a glimmer in their eyes and say, "You know what? I don't have to be limited by others' guidelines either. I don't have to stop here. I can push against that. I can bang against that. I can ignore that."

So that's how I have gotten people together, and that's how I have helped them to do things that they didn't think were possible. People discover their own boundless potential, learning that the perceived boundaries need not define their reality. Through leading by example, I've fostered environments where the unthinkable becomes attainable, inspiring people and teams to exceed not just expectations but their own imaginations.

Chapter 9

Thriving Amidst Flux

Mike Tomlin, the coach of the Pittsburgh Steelers, has a philosophy he's established with the team: "The standard is the standard." What I believe Tomlin means by that is that regardless of who is in the lineup, they are expected to maintain the Steelers' high standards. It doesn't matter if you're the backup or the backup to the backup—when you get in the game, you must, at a minimum, maintain the standard. The players may change, but the standard never does (change).

My father had a very similar mindset, although his rendition of the mantra often left out a clear articulation or definition of what the standard was. In my father's mind, I was what he called a "social experiment." I recall him sharing that with me as a young adult. A social experiment. What does that mean, exactly? And who says that to their child? It was a very curious thing, at best, for a parent to say to their child.

However, as I grew, those words brought a lot of clarity to me regarding the things he did, the way that he did them, and all the things he didn't do. I talked in an earlier chapter about my parents, but it bears repeating: I was raised by tiger parents. Tiger parents on steroids, to be precise. Anyone familiar with that concept might think it applies predominantly to Asian parents, but my experience suggests it is a universal trait of parents who have soaring, non-negotiable standards and expectations of their children. Tiger parents will not compromise those standards or relax or reduce those standards in any sort of way, just like Tomlin of the Steelers. The standard is the standard, and that is exactly how I was raised. My childhood was a rigorous proving ground created by parents who espoused a relentless pursuit of excellence. The bar was celestial, and the consequences for faltering were severe. The unique social experiment part was that my parents didn't tell me what to do; instead, they expected me to figure it out and held me accountable for what I did and did not do.

They expected me to get the right things done the right way, and there were consequences for failing to meet those expectations.

I wish that my father had been more balanced. I knew when I did wrong. I knew when I didn't hit the standard. It, however, would have been valuable to receive some positive affirmation of the effort I put in rather than only hearing about it when I fell short. Instead, life was a relentless cycle: achieve, then ascend immediately to the next precipice. Consequently, I was never allowed to get comfortable or become complacent. When I hit the standard, there were no slaps on the back or words of acknowledgment. Instead, I would be picked up and tossed into even deeper water, where I was expected to figure it all out on my own. I was never allowed to experience consistency or predictability. Comfort was an alien concept; I was perpetually tasked with deciphering life's puzzles sans guidance. Every minute of every day brought some new challenge, and I was expected to rise up and meet those challenges under my own power. Life was one big, perpetual "FITFO" exercise. Figure it the (expletive) out, son.

The significance, value, and noteworthiness of those experiences lie in the fact that they taught me how to be an independent thinker. It taught me how to think critically and how to sort through problems, situations, and challenges of which I had little to no knowledge or prior experience. "I don't know" or "I give up" were completely unacceptable responses and outcomes. Winning was the only way to avoid those aforementioned severe consequences. I learned how to work effectively under extreme pressure and stress. I learned to make decisions, and perhaps most importantly, I learned how to work through ambiguity. In the absence of predetermined rules, structure, precedent, or guidance, I learned how to THRIVE!

I learned that life is a constant state of flux. We are always evolving. Change is an inevitable aspect of life and of living. I learned how to be the architect, orchestrator, and executor of the change that I wanted in my life. By embracing the opportunity to seize that responsibility, I also became an empowered author of my own destiny and story. Today, that understanding is hard-wired in my circuitry; I embrace change with every fiber of my being. I seek it. I want it, and most importantly, I initiate and drive it.

Working in Charlotte, the birthplace of NASCAR, I learned a clever colloquialism that also applies to this idea of constant change. In NASCAR, they say, "If you ain't rubbing, you ain't racing," which resonated deeply. Victory demands a bruising dance with risk, where the safety of the status quo is a veil that obscures the path to greatness. True racers—and I count myself among them—hunger for the friction of the fray, the daring maneuvers that etch our presence into the annals of time. In other words, winners are always pushing boundaries and putting themselves out there. If you want to succeed, if you want to win, you can't simply go around that track 400 times and bring the car home without a scratch. You must race. You must take risks. You must push yourself. You must tighten your turns and force the other car into the spot you want, even if it means scraping the paint job, denting a fender, or worse.

With every heartbeat, I champion change as a path to winning; I seek it in the alleys of comfort, and I craft it in the workshops of content. The lessons from my youth have metastasized into an ethos where change is not just inevitable but essential and sought—it is the currency of the bold, the script of the intrepid. My quest is a ceaseless race, one that implores me to scorch the tracks of complacency and herald an epoch of uncharted excellence. It's about leaving an indelible mark—a legacy not for personal triumph but for the collective ascendancy of all. As I stand poised, ready to channel these formative crucibles into presidential leadership, my gaze is set firmly on the horizon. We won't merely navigate the tumultuous seas of our time; we will harness them, riding the waves of change to shape a world emboldened by our shared audacity to race, to risk, to revolutionize.

I am not here to maintain the status quo.

I am here to race.

I am here to win.

I am here to make this place better—for everyone.

Championing Transformation: The Journey to Excellence

To achieve consistency, we must consistently encounter and surmount challenges and strive for continuous progression and improvement. Standing still is not an option in a world defined by constant evolution and change. My philosophy aligns with the proactive mindset and counterintuitive wisdom of my mentor, Rick Pitino: "If it ain't broke, break it." This principle means we never settle or fall victim to the illusion of the status quo. Instead, we always strive to improve and prepare for whatever the future holds. The status quo, however momentarily good it might be, is tomorrow's failure.

Everything around us is evolving. Everything around you is in a constant state of flux. If you are attempting to stand pat, you're losing ground—minute by minute, day by day, week by week, year by year.

This concept of evolution permeates everything; standing still equates to regression. This principle has been my guidepost; if something can be improved, I will not hesitate to dismantle and reconstruct it better. My role is to prepare us for any upcoming challenges, ensuring that complacency doesn't hinder our readiness for the constant waves of change.

Metrics have always been a cornerstone of my approach, embodying the wisdom of the famous educator, author, and management consultant Peter Drucker: "If you can't measure it, you can't manage it." My professional experience has honed my appreciation for metrics, as they are vital for understanding current positioning and guiding improvement. Without measurement, managing progress becomes an insurmountable task.

My leadership style is balanced between the human touch and objective, fact-based management. Transparency about what is working and not is paramount, as it enables my team and I to witness the real-time impact of our actions. Moreover, we ask ourselves, what value are our efforts creating and adding to our overarching goals?

I used to enjoy a show called *The Biggest Loser;* a reality TV program focused on weight loss. Contestants, who typically struggled with obesity, competed to lose the most weight through rigorous diet and exercise programs. Trainers, nutritionists, and medical professionals guided contestants throughout the process, and the goal of the show was to promote healthy weight loss and lifestyle changes while also offering emotional support and motivation to people struggling with their weight. At the end of each season, the contestant who achieved the highest percentage of weight loss was declared the winner.

I appreciated learning how people grapple with their bodies and come to understand that their weight issues often started with issues they had in their heads and their relationship to food and what food meant to them. The scale was a measure of the efforts and their understanding. Put in terms of a balanced scorecard—if you waited to get on the scale to know where you were trending—it was already too late. If you slept well, did your workouts consistently and with intensity, passion, and focus, switched things up, and continually added new challenges, thresholds, and new expectations for your body, you were almost never surprised when you stepped on the scale. You were already aware of all your leading measures—your workout regimen, your caloric intake, for example—and if you kept them in the positive, the readout on the scale was rarely a surprise.

I devised a comprehensively detailed scorecard system. This comprehensive tool was not just an abstract concept; it, in some ways, mirrored the real-world scenario of *The Biggest Loser*. Our scorecard indicated the status of our leading efforts; if the measures were positive, success was not a surprise but an expectation.

The scorecard my team and I created was over 100 pages long. Very impressive. This artifact was a 100-page Louisville slugger because, boom, I could show you in an instant what we were doing, what we were achieving, how people were spending their time, and what value that investment was creating for the company. It was crucial to reversing our direction from wastefully crashing to effectively racing forward. We knew where we needed to focus more effort. Soon, we were winning.

We were operating in an agile fashion that no one else in the firm had previously achieved.

An innovative tool christened "The Master Performance Indicator" was born out of the need for a succinct representation of our complex scorecard. It distilled five critical metrics into one figure, offering an at-a-glance view of our technological organization's health. This single number emerged as a shining testament to the efficacy of our work—a diamond born from the intense scrutiny of our extensive efforts.

I share this story to help reveal who I am and what I bring to the table in a leadership role. It illustrates the commitment and innovation I bring to measuring, analyzing, and displaying in a quantitative fashion what progress looks like. Equally important, it reveals the core of who I am. This is at the core of how I run the businesses that I work for and the businesses that I've created. It's how I measure my life. It's how I measure myself. It's a core part of my DNA.

Things are going to change. My DNA is encoded with the tenacity to architect and oversee change, grounded in the high standards set forth by my upbringing. As Mike Tomlin aptly asserts, "The standard is the standard," and I stand ready to uphold, evolve, and elevate those standards at every opportunity.

Queue the Black Swans

Transparency and metrics are essential, not merely for charting progress but also for uncovering vulnerabilities. The journey is punctuated with bumps, stumbles, and falls, particularly at the outset. It is imperative to acknowledge these stumbles openly. The aversion to admitting failure within government circles must evolve; to fail is to strive, learn, and ultimately improve. To paraphrase the words of Thomas Edison, failing simply means you succeed at finding one more way something won't work.

When you genuinely race and race as hard as you can to consistently win, you are going to be the victim—and I hate using that word—but you're going to be the victim of unintended consequences. You will create consequences that you didn't anticipate. Encountering unintended consequences is an inescapable aspect of pioneering efforts. Actually, it is an unavoidable fact of life (e.g., the COVID-19 global pandemic).

There are going to be black swans. Let me explain. The term "black swan" originated in ancient Europe when people believed all swans were white because that was the only kind they had ever seen. A black swan came to represent how universal beliefs can be disproven by a single incident, like the arrival of a black swan. Nassim Nicholas Taleb, a prominent author, essayist, and former options trader known for his work on randomness and risk, used the term to describe unexpected and impactful events that disrupt established understanding and impact history, life, science, and finance. The concept symbolizes and underscores the limitations of human foresight and knowledge.

The COVID-19 pandemic exemplified a black swan event. No one could have anticipated it, although there were signs. During his presidency, George W. Bush responded to SARS (Severe Acute Respiratory Syndrome) in the early 2000s with an increased focus on pandemic preparedness. In 2005, he announced the National Strategy for Pandemic Influenza, aiming to enhance preparedness for a potential influenza pandemic. During Obama's term, the swine flu emerged as a global pandemic, and the administration declared a public health emergency, allocating funds for vaccine development and implementing measures to mitigate the spread of the virus.

That said, was our country prepared for COVID-19? Not really. This reflects an American cultural tendency to prioritize the immediate over long-term strategy often. This attitude empowers us with a sense of urgency but also hampers us from creating and following a long-term strategic plan. But those black swans are out there, and we've got to be ready to anticipate them and react to them.

My administration will prioritize metric-driven transparency and acknowledge that setbacks are inevitable and, in some cases, unavoidable. When facing them, we will adapt and continue to climb. Observing the rapid learning of children—how they swiftly transition from faltering steps to graceful strides—serves as a reminder that learning involves overcoming falls. When you watch children, it's amazing how quickly they learn things. One day, they're stumbling, bumbling, mumbling, and the next day they're just gliding around. What the hell happened? How did that happen? It isn't that they possess any sort of magical power.

In his book, *Outliers*, Malcolm Gladwell suggested that achieving a high level of expertise in any field typically requires around 10,000 hours of dedicated practice. Practice and immersion over time are crucial to achieve mastery of something. Gladwell used Tiger Woods as an example. From a very young age, Woods showed an astonishing dedication to practicing golf. Woods' early exposure to golf, combined with his intense practice regimen and the guidance of his father, played a crucial role in his remarkable success as a professional golfer.

It isn't just that people like Woods practiced a lot. They do more than practice. They immerse themselves in their craft. Even as a child, Woods was sketching out the arc of various chip shots in his elementary school notebooks. The sketches look like something a mathematician might draw to prove a theorem or something. For people like Tiger Woods, time stands still when they are engaged in their craft. Artists call it "flow." When time is trickling past the rest of us, an hour feels like a minute for them. It races and stands still, all at once, because they are completely immersed in what they're doing.

As we age or engage in less impassioned pursuits, we tend to forget that stumbling and falling is part of the mastery process. There isn't a child in the world who didn't crawl before walking and fall while taking their first steps. It's part of the process. But for some reason, as we get older, we equate falling, tripping, and stumbling with making mistakes rather than viewing them as following a process to greater skill.

Tony Robbins, a great motivational speaker, talks about this. To Robbins, falling is not a mistake. Failure is not a mistake. It's part of the process. Without falling, you'll never walk. Without walking, you'll never run. Without running, you'll never win the race.

In technology, we call the process "failing fast." In fact, the term is so common that it's become a cliché. In technology, it's all: fail fast, fail fast, fail fast. But nobody wants to fail because there's a stigma attached to failure. There's a whole negative aura and energy attached to failure. So, let's be clear: failing is part of the process. Failure is knowledge, and, as Sir Francis Bacon famously noted in the 17th century, "Knowledge is power." In Bacon's mind, the phrase emphasizes the belief that knowledge equips us with the ability to understand, influence, and control our surroundings, leading us to empowerment and success.

We need to begin failing fast if we are going to succeed in changing life on this planet and correct the course of issues such as climate change. Let's stop pretending that the warming climate is a natural process occurring outside our influence. We humans are at the center of it. But just as we caused it with an overabundance of greenhouse gasses and the decimation of natural resources, we also have the ability to find a solution. However, we need to do it quickly. Climate change is not going to reverse itself without our influence.

We have big rocks to climb. We have big boulders to smash. Almost every week, it seems, we experience different hundred-year climatological events, such as tropical storm Hillary or Hurricane Maria, which caused catastrophic damage to Puerto Rico and created a humanitarian crisis there as well as in the U.S. Virgin Islands and the mainland of the United States. It was the most destructive hurricane in U.S. history, but it's only one of a parade of historically devastating storms that is literally reshaping the coastal contours of our planet.

And if we don't stop, if we don't do something extraordinary to change our course or alter our path, things are going to be incredibly bad for us.

The urgency to act is unparalleled. As a committed leader, I aim to race toward change to confront the bumps head-on. Through new metrics and transparent assessments, we'll observe our progress in real time, adjusting swiftly and effectively to ensure a sustainable future.

Running for the Bus

I grew up in a predominantly African American section of Pittsburgh. One aspect of my childhood was marked by a seemingly perpetual rush to catch the next bus to predominantly white schools across town. With each hurried sprint, I embodied a tussle between optimism and resignation; even as my body urged me to relent, my mind would push me to persist. It became something of a metaphor for life: the optimist in me racing against the darkness and never-ending whispering doubts.

Despite this internal struggle, I never failed to keep running. I would refuse to succumb or surrender to the temptation to stop running or to even slow down. That was the optimist in me. However, did not keep me from consciously acknowledging the notion that I was going to fail because that was the most likely outcome. So why am I running in the first place, and why am I running so hard? That was the darkness. And it would go back and forth like that. The optimist told me to run harder. The dark side told me to slow down. My father once said to me, "You know what your problem is? You're too dumb to quit." I know that he did not mean that as a badge of honor, but that tenacity is one of my most coveted superpowers.

This internal battle has shaped the way I've led my life and inspired others.

I expected the first Republican debate of the 2024 campaign to be an interesting experience, but I was alarmed at what I saw. It wasn't a debate; it was little more than a chaotic shouting match. It was just a bunch of voices yelling at one another, not saying much of anything of substance regarding how they were going to move this country and the world forward. I heard candidates talking about how the US needs to stop focusing on everyone else or helping anyone else so we could focus on ourselves. This, I found absolutely incredible. It was as though that candidate had not lived through the recent pandemic.

There is no us and them. The pandemic proved that we all share this planet. What we do here affects people elsewhere. And the things the people out there do matter to this country. We can't go our own way. It's not that simple. The problems are more complex than that approach acknowledges.

We are challenged to rise above and beyond simple-minded insular thinking, to cultivate proficiency in collaboration and shared progress. Doubts will be cast on our capacity to succeed to "catch the bus," so to speak. Yet, it's in these moments that the optimist in me confronts the darkness with defiance: acknowledging the likelihood of failure as the impetus to strive harder.

There will be people inside and out who will look at us and say, "What are we doing? We can't make it. We're not going to make that bus." That's where it's up to me. That is when the optimist in me tells the darkness, "You know, you're probably right. We probably won't make that bus. BUT we can't afford NOT to make that bus. We better run harder. We better run faster. We better be smarter. There is no shortcut in this race, but there is an alternative path. Is there something we can do that will help us be more effective, efficient, capable, and stronger? Of course there is, because we're making that bus."

I always make the bus. I hate that I put myself or find myself in those situations where I must run in the first place, but once the challenge is before me, I won't stop running. I just run faster, and I FITFO (figure it the %#*! out!) how to catch that bus. There is a proverb that says, "Fortune favors the brave." Sometimes the bus is a little late. Sometimes, there's a long line of people waiting to get on. So, the bus is delayed, and you run up to the door, and you're the last one to board before the door folds closed behind you.

Fortune favors the brave. So, let's be brave.

By being brave, we can find our fortune. And as for legacy, it's not for me to muse upon. My focus is on the present, on being brave, and meeting each challenge head-on. Legacy is crafted by actions, not intentions.

It Is Our Legacy

This book is about legacy—however, it is not my legacy. It is about our legacy. As I look at the challenges we face, legacy, as defined within these pages, transcends the individual—it's a collective heritage we craft through action. I pen these words not to etch my own mark—this audacious, preposterous thing—but to ignite a fire within *us*, to provoke action before opportunities to effect meaningful change become mere echoes of regret. It's about transforming "could have been" into the reality of what we will achieve.

So, this narrative isn't just mine. It's the tale of a lone, unconventional dance on a mountaintop, sparking curiosity, then emulation, then innovation. It's about a point in time when someone started dancing on a mountain in an awkward way—half-clothed or poorly clothed, perhaps—doing something no one understood, causing people to ask, "Why the hell is that person doing that here? We don't do that here. That looks really unseemly."

Yet I keep doing it until someone feels compelled to say, "You know what? That dance looks kind of interesting. He's not doing it particularly well, but maybe I can do it better. I can get out there and maybe show him a move or two." And that person gets out there and starts dancing. And others say, "You know what? That actually kind of looks interesting. The music is good. That first guy's rhythm is off, but those other people know how to move. Maybe I can build up to that and add to it. I can take a little bit of what he's doing and add a little bit of my own flavor to it."

And the next thing you know, you have a movement. You have momentum. You have strength. You have people doing something different, dynamic, positive, impactful, and valuable that is pushing the boundaries of what they thought was normal or acceptable. In this way, we change the world.

It was early in my career that I initially learned the concept of a balanced scorecard. I have since taken that skill, capability, and formality to every place I worked thereafter because it is so powerful and impactful. We transparently measured progress, but we also evolved the measures. If you have leading measures and you pull certain levers until the marginal utility of change is no longer worth the energy it takes to continue pulling, you come up with a different measure with a different lever. That process drives more change, faster change, and more impactful and valuable change.

We kept doing that, and our program evolved dramatically. We went from one of the lowest-margin businesses in the company to one of the highest-margin businesses in less than five years. The change was driven by the work that we were doing in my technology space.

Moreover, our people have evolved. Other places sought our people, and we became exporters of talent. In fact, we encouraged our people to leave—to take what they'd learned with us and bring it to other divisions so that they could benefit. We were actually pushing our talent out of the nest and watching them fly. We said, "Go. You can't stay here. You can't be complacent or comfortable. Go change the company. Be apostles of what we have done and sow the seeds of change and excellence in other parts of the firm." To other organizations within the company, we said, "You have a big thing you want to accomplish? We have people who can do those kinds of things." In this way, we helped to push the entire company forward.

Albert Einstein talked about quantum entanglement, how two things, despite the time and space that separates them, can be manipulated from a distance. I believe the world and the universe are a very, very connected place. Those things that I was learning on the job and in those organizations are exactly the skills that I intend to employ in this endeavor to bring change.

The entanglement Einstein pondered, the interconnectedness of all, mirrors our shared journey. As we embrace the struggle and the missteps, we simultaneously embrace the evolution and the climb. And together, we'll forge a legacy not just of individual triumphs but of collective ascent to excellence.

Chapter 10

A Coalition of the Willing

The chapter title, while echoing some biblical resonances, is definitely not a prelude to religious discourse or a religious treatise of any kind. Rather, it is an acknowledgment of my faith and my roots in a family deeply committed to its Pentecostal beliefs.

This narrative is about harnessing collective will. Hence, a coalition of the willing refers to the times we find ourselves united—as individuals or in groups—by a common sense of purpose and a shared mental model of what constitutes success. We have shared objectives and a commitment to those goals that rise above all else. And when we have that, we can move mountains. The world is full of examples of positive and not-so positive events caused by a gathering of like-minded souls. One example, sadly, occurred on September 11, 2001. That was the awful day when nineteen like-minded people changed life as we know it on this planet. Nineteen people with the same ideas, goals, and purpose changed the lives of billions of people around the globe—not just on that day but for years to come.

There are, however, many examples of profoundly positive change, as well. Transformative figures like Mandela and Gandhi, whose staunch resolve and daily acts of dedication altered the course of history, have inspired many others who have taken the reins of their message—people of deep faith and commitment who are resolute in what they believe, committed to their goals and values, and willing to take action every day to bring about the change they want to see.

So, there is power in just one person starting what can become a movement.

Rosa Parks. One action—that declaration of sitting on that bus and asserting at that moment that "I'm not going to move." It was one action that catalyzed a movement that changed the world.

I have seen this so many times, and I have seen it in my own family. When my grandfather decided to start a church, he transformed his Pittsburgh neighborhood. His vision is being carried on by the extraordinary congregation that has taken the reins from my grandfather and is advancing his mission forward into the future.

We saw it during the pandemic when schools closed. Schools are a source of many things in the United States; schools often provide meals to children whose families can't afford to eat properly. When that source of good nutrition disappeared during the pandemic, we saw people pitching in and gathering food to ensure these children continued to receive nutritional meals that helped them grow and develop—vividly showcasing humanity's capacity to effectuate positive change through collective action. We absolutely can make positive things happen. We just must be consciously committed to doing so. We must make it the norm. People must think of it as their responsibility. We must be focused, mindful, and intentional about it. We can't afford to quibble about receiving credit or recognition or debating about whose idea it was. We just must get it done.

This text, articulating the rationale for my presidential aspiration, is predicated on the urgency of the work before us—to steer our nation and safeguard our planet and its inhabitants for posterity. That said, as I have previously stated–several times–this mission is not about me. My voice is a conduit for this call to action, seeking to assemble a cadre of aligned advocates. The aspiration here is to initiate a tide of change that reshapes our shared existence for the broader good, transcending individual benefit. I feel intensely compelled to do something, irrespective of whether I ever see the White House.

I don't necessarily need that presidential platform to design and create sustained, positive change. Not having that platform is not an excuse to do nothing. However, I do think we need someone in the White House to execute the things I'm outlining here, to have the perspective I've outlined in this book, and to be committed above all else to moving this world forward in a way that makes life as we know it different and better for the collective, not just for a few.

My voice is giving rise to that. My voice is saying I need one more like-minded recruit, and then another, and then another. As we gather this group of like-minded people, small at first but no less powerful, we can and will change the world. There's no doubt in my mind. We must. The alternative is unacceptable. Failure is not an option. Apathy is completely unacceptable.

This movement doesn't require an army, at least not at first. It doesn't require a movement. It takes two or three to start, and when these folks gather, mountains can be moved.

As my own narrative unfolds, I desire it to reflect a legacy of action—a testament to standing up, collaborating, and effecting change. It is a commitment to face doubts and fears head-on, confront and dispel them, and progress triumphantly towards something that is collectively positive.

I firmly believe two or three more people feel that way, and I intend to find them, collaborate with them, and get some things done with them. You can insert your own expletive in there anywhere you'd like for emphasis. I absolutely do have my moments of doubts and occasional fears, it's true; I would not be a "Dark Optimist" if I didn't. However, my overwhelming conviction is not to be deterred or held back by any of those things. Acknowledging my fears and doubts allows me to confront them and deal with them. It allows me to address them, embrace them, rebuke them, hold them at bay, and ultimately, push beyond them.

I feel so enormously triumphant to be here in Chapter 10. I am near the end of this process, and despite how preposterous, audacious, and illogical this part of my journey may be, I firmly believe someone will pick up this book, become inspired, and see the opportunity to make a difference. And when that happens, change blossoms. Change becomes inevitable.

The title of this book comes from a story about a child and their enjoyment of and fascination with circus elephants. He was awed by their size majesty and the fact that they were being controlled by a relatively small man wielding a chair and a whip. Circus elephants are conditioned from birth to ignore their physical stature in the world, and this allows them to be controlled by trainers who are a fraction of their size. However, if or when elephants recognize what they are, they recognize their power. Moreover, when they come together, they see the great power of the herd, and they recognize an even greater power. They realize they have nothing to lose by acting differently than the circumstances in which they find themselves. The analogy of circus elephants—shackled not by their physicality but by mental conditioning—serves as a metaphor for our own potential awakening to the power inherent within us and magnified in unison. This story, this reality that I'm authoring, is a manifestation of empowerment, an invitation for a collective ascendance to massive, meaningful change.

Change is coming. A revolution is coming.

I have nothing to lose by authoring this and speaking this reality into existence. Power starts with the one and can grow exponentially with this gathering.

Embracing Empathy

The positive examples I share typically originate with people who have a profound sense of empathy. Although I'm naturally an empathetic person, my compassion was significantly heightened after I endured a life-altering motorcycle accident.

I had always wanted a motorcycle, and several years ago, I purchased one. I took to it immediately, and in short order, I felt as though I had been riding all my life. In retrospect, I was riding far above my experience level. One serene Sunday, July morning, when the roads of northeastern Pennsylvania were quiet, I lost the back end of the bike on a particularly challenging stretch of road. The bike went down with my leg trapped under it. My body rolled, but my leg did not, and I sustained severe damage to my leg, largely centered around my knee. Only the fact that I was wearing the best available safety gear saved me from a far more dramatic and possibly fatal result.

I had only just started a new job in New York City; however, my employer was understanding and stood by me through several weeks of recovery. During my convalescence, which spanned multiple operations and weeks of excruciating therapy, I not only grappled with physical recovery but also with a profound reassessment of life's fragility.

I had a newfound appreciation for the challenges faced by people with disabilities. I had a newfound understanding of how a person's life can change in a split second. I had new insight into how vulnerable we all are. Life is a gift not to be squandered or treated with cavalier overconfidence. Strangely, I did not come to think we must live in fear; we just need to never take life and opportunities for granted. We must savor them.

Empathy, thus deepened, has become a cornerstone of how I engage with the world. It's a realization that life's worth is immeasurable, and the compassion shown to me during my recovery became a crucial lifeline. This ethos extends into my view on leadership and change: acknowledging that genuine empathy must be coupled with decisive action.

Jamie Dimon, the CEO of JPMorgan Chase, likes to say, "Visions without execution are merely dreams." Those words resonate deeply with me. This philosophy is crucial as we forge a path forward, recognizing that the shared conviction and commitment of a 'coalition of the willing' is potent, but it must manifest in concrete actions. It's not enough to share a vision; we must live it, enact it, and ensure it withstands the trials of both scrutiny and adversity.

People sometimes ask, "How do you strike a balance between the zeal of a united coalition and staying on course?" It's a good question. There must be a moral compass.

In crafting my approach, I meticulously outline my intentions, continuously asking myself about the purpose, the significance, and the ethical boundaries of my actions. This continuously reflective practice ensures that my zeal never loses sight of righteousness, aiming for transformative change that is both profound and positive.

Even in the face of significant global unrest, we see so many great examples of positive, nonviolent change. Examples include Greta Thunberg, the Swedish environmental activist who has gained international recognition for her efforts to address climate change. In 2018, at the age of 15, she started skipping school on Fridays to protest outside the Swedish parliament, calling for stronger action on climate change. Her "School Strike for Climate" evolved into a global movement known as "Fridays for Future" that subsequently involved students around the world.

Then there is Malala Yousafzai, who gained international recognition for her advocacy of education for girls in her native Swat Valley in Pakistan, where the local Taliban had at times banned girls from attending school. Malala spoke out against these restrictions and promoted the importance of education for girls. In 2012, Malala was shot in the head by a Taliban gunman to silence her advocacy for girls' education. She survived and courageously continued her activism all over the world.

These are but two whose actions vividly exemplify the impact of individual resolve and the ripple effect of standing firm in one's convictions. Their stories inspire not just contemplation and awe but action, prompting millions to support causes and engage with movements that align with our deepest values.

In this era of fleeting attention spans, where the morning's news is passé by the afternoon, sustaining a movement is challenging. Maintaining momentum demands that we keep our narratives alive across numerous platforms. We must consistently seize and win the day. And the best way to do that is by winning—winning big and winning small. We must remain keenly aware of what we're doing and how we're doing it. We must bombard our audience with news of our accomplishments and our ongoing challenges, utilizing every technological tool at our disposal to continuously engage and re-engage public interest. We spend untold hours every day on our phones. Our watches relay messages, and soon, our ear pods will. Before long, special optical devices will make an array of information available to us wherever we happen to be (that is something that is already happening). We must keep our message alive on all these platforms, continually helping people understand the mission, what's expected of them, and the next thing we hope to accomplish. This is the challenge of our time: not only to capture attention but also to sustain it long enough to effect real change.

We all seem to have the attention span of gnats. Securing someone's attention and maintaining their interest and focus is profoundly difficult. We must leverage these devices and platforms in a crowded world to keep our collective on message and excited about what's going on. We must keep them centered on the work that we're doing and the impact it's having.

In this journey, my story is not just about leadership but about fostering a community of action, a congregation of individuals empowered by shared values and a common goal. It is here, in the confluence of empathy and action, that true legacy is formed—not merely through words but through the enduring impact of our deeds.

Dark Optimists, LET'S CHANGE THE WORLD!

Chapter 11

Technology and Leadership

Throughout this book, I've emphasized and spoken about the transformative potential of technology in shaping our economy and governance. Allow me to give you some additional perspective on what leads me to this position.

I graduated from Boston University with a degree in finance and went on to get a master's degree in economics and urban policy and then an MBA. Originally, my career aspirations were set against the energetic backdrop of New York, where I aimed to make my mark as a financial trader before venturing into politics—first as mayor, then potentially the presidency. Law school was on my radar. However, financial considerations nudged me toward immediate employment. As time passed, law became less appealing, and technology caught my imagination. My technology epiphany occurred at Bankers Trust, within the commercial bank operations sector. There, I quickly recognized how technology could significantly streamline tasks, reducing reliance on manual labor. For me, success came to be defined as eliminating the very job that I was doing. In other words, when you no longer needed me, I had achieved success. I maintain that attitude today. How can we make technology work for us rather than the other way around?

After leaving the financial industry for a time to work on a startup, I returned to the corporate world to focus on technology. That's when my career in technology began. What I brought to the field was a business view of how-to best leverage technology to achieve and enhance business objectives and drive profitable business outcomes. I understood how to build sustainable and competitive advantages, leverage technology to create differentiating kinds of capabilities and opportunities and create experiences that would attract and retain customers and clients. That was my personal value proposition in the field of technology, and I've been highly successful at that.

By the early 2000s, I believed technology was going to be ubiquitous with life itself on this planet. I came upon a book by a futurist, Ray Kurzweil, titled *The Singularity is Near*, which talks about the amalgamation of human biology with human technology to create something new. In Kurzweil's view, progress is not as linear as we think; instead, the 21st century could deliver the equivalent of a thousand years' worth of growth. According to Kurzweil, by 2030, humans won't be smart enough to invent anything; machines will have access to their source code and will be creating for and by themselves enhancements and new capabilities and new functionalities that we won't be able to participate in because we are simply not smart enough. At least not until we begin augmenting ourselves with technology.

In discussions about the future of warfare and aviation, I've come across some compelling opinions regarding the F-35 fighter jet. It's said that this could be the last fighter jet that humans will ever personally fly. Advancements in technology suggest that future aircraft will likely be unmanned and more technologically integrated than anything we currently deploy. This shift toward automation and enhanced technology isn't confined to military applications; it permeates all sectors of our lives.

We are on an unstoppable journey toward a future where technology is at the forefront of everything we do. Given this trajectory, I urge young people, regardless of their field of study or passion, to embrace technology as part of their education. It's clear that future careers, in every discipline, will be intertwined with technological advancements.

The book *Wired for War* by P. W. Singer posits an intriguing perspective on the origins of significant innovations in human history, suggesting that many of these advancements have arisen from the crucible of conflict. This view, while debatable, highlights the undeniable impact that military needs have had on technological progress. From the creation of the internet, which was developed under the auspices of the Defense Advanced Research Projects Agency (DARPA) and the Department of Defense, to the development of GPS and autonomous vehicles, conflict has indeed been a catalyst for technological advancements. The Global Positioning System and driverless cars sprang from war and the research efforts of our government and defense apparatus.

The current administration, as have others in the past, has acknowledged the crucial role of the government in fostering technological innovation, particularly in recognizing that future breakthroughs essential for national advancement and security often stem from well-funded and directed government research. The challenge now is clearly defining the role of government in this process moving forward.

But what does that look like? That is the critical question before us.

Fostering Technological Progress: The Endless Frontier Act

The Endless Frontier Act represents a strategic initiative to establish a national technological agency distinct from the Department of Defense (DOD), DARPA, and the energy departments. In my humble opinion, that sounds like an excellent idea. The agency's primary focus will be on integrating advanced technology into our daily lives to enhance national development and outpace global competitors like China. While the Biden administration has championed this separation of technology from defense and energy, this perspective is not new. It is, however, critical in driving technological research, investment, and widespread application.

Achieving consensus on this matter is complicated, difficult, and fraught with significant challenges. Intentions that appear to be noble often stall and dissolve into inaction due to conflicting viewpoints among key factions. These include the freedom faction, which advocates minimal government interference; the flourish faction, which supports technological advancements to boost national prosperity; and the fairness faction, which argues for a global approach to technological development, emphasizing cooperation rather than competition with countries like Russia and China.

The pandemic provided a vivid illustration of the rapid advancements in science and technology. It was fascinating to watch our country participate in the global race to develop and/or secure access to a vaccine. And once a vaccine was available, observe how the ethical questions about whether advancements should be hoarded nationally or shared globally, especially given the interconnected nature of global health. Should we have hoarded those vaccines for ourselves? Clearly, we needed them due in part to the fact that we were suffering the greatest number of deaths of any country in the world. The pandemic was a very stark reminder that we all share one planet. We are all connected, and things that were happening in other parts of the world were always going to impact us being safe here. I can, in many ways, appreciate a fairness faction that says we should perhaps think more globally and broader than just ourselves.

Looking ahead, any administration I am part of will prioritize technology as a fundamental pillar to shape our policies and achieve desired outcomes. There is a pressing need to harness technology not for surveillance or control but to genuinely improve people's lives across the country. We are currently at a pivotal moment in the evolution of AI and autonomous technologies. These tools are now capable of operating independently in critical areas, such as military applications, without human oversight, driven by the necessity to stay ahead in international defense technologies.

Prominent leaders and voices in technology, like Elon Musk and Bill Gates, are sounding warning bells about the potential risk AI poses, and I understand why. There are some perspectives being voiced that call AI an existential threat to human life. The velocity of the advancements being made is, at the very least, surprising. It's the lily pad analogy again; if you're sitting there watching the pond, nothing appears to be happening. But if you go away for a month, upon your return, you will find the pond covered in lily pads. That's due to exponential growth. AI development is accelerating at such a pace that we may no longer be able to control or even guide it.

We were not talking about AI this way a year or so ago, and next year, we will be talking about it in a completely different manner. That's how quickly things are moving. It is quite possible that we may be approaching a point where we won't be driving it, teaching it, or managing it. Today, these large AI models are created—the algorithms are created, and they devour information from humans. It won't be long before these models begin to look for information on their own and explore their own sense of what the information is telling them and the outcomes and the conclusions they should reach as a result of the information they're ingesting. And these models are relentless. They don't sleep. They don't take vacations. They don't stop. Hence, it is critical to incorporate diverse and inclusive perspectives in the creation of these AI models and their governing algorithms.

Harnessing AI for Good

Artificial intelligence offers transformative potential across a variety of sectors, including the judicial system. A pressing challenge we face is the overwhelming influx of asylum seekers at our borders. The sheer volume of cases necessitates a modern solution to expedite the adjudication process.

Companies like Google, OpenAI, IBM, Microsoft, and Meta are at the forefront of developing AI models that could be integrated into government platforms. These models could be augmented to have the capability to process asylum cases swiftly—potentially adjudicating tens of thousands of cases weekly and millions annually. Imagine if we incorporated AI, significantly reducing the time spent per case from months or years to mere minutes. Moreover, to ensure fairness, accuracy, and consistency, a human-led, random sampling of AI decisions could be implemented. This would serve as a check to align AI decisions with human judgment and ensure they meet our legal and ethical standards.

Assuming and ensuring the algorithms are properly written and the models are properly trained, the AI decisions would be better than those we as humans would make, at a minimum, from a consistency and timeliness perspective. We could potentially eliminate significant systemic bias. Additionally, these models don't get tired. They are not going to grow old. They are not going to retire (unless we decide to retire them). And we could amicably and humanely get through millions of cases. The opportunity to use AI to adjudicate these cases is an opportunity we should explore now. Forget about building a wall. We can adjudicate tens of thousands of cases at the drop of a hat.

Leveraging AI in our judicial system doesn't have to stop there. It is a proven fact that there is an extraordinary level of bias in our judicial system today, from how bail is allocated, judged, and awarded, to sentencing. Why couldn't we leverage AI to better inform judges about what fair and unbiased decisions look like? We know biases drive mass incarceration in our country today.

The opportunities to leverage technology go on and on.

Let's talk about gun responsibility. We can build weapons that recognize their legal owners, eliminating the opportunity for these weapons to be used by people who were not properly vetted. That's not going to solve the entire problem of gun violence, but it would improve some of what is wrong with gun ownership in this country.

The changes wrought by AI will drive massive social and economic upheaval in this country, much like the Industrial Revolution, but at an accelerated pace. We must anticipate what that means, what it looks like, and how we are going to manage that transformational change at all levels. The wealth gap is likely to grow, and those at the lower strata of our economic social ladder are likely to be the most impacted by the advent of technology and the use of technology by our government. We need to get ahead of what that looks like, what it means, and what we are going to do about it.

The underlying algorithms that AI models are built on cannot be a black box. We must have transparency and the ability to access them, interrogate them, and understand them. We must know how these models are constructed and trained. We must be able to see the model work through the questions it's fed, the information it's fed, and the outcomes it delivers.

It's almost like being in school and solving problems. You turn in your work with your answer so the teacher can see how you arrived at your conclusion. Only then can you see the reasoning behind the solution. If the answer is correct but the reasoning is incorrect, you've got a problem. If the answer is off slightly, but the approach was correct, you deserve some credit. If the answer makes sense and your reasoning is sound, but you used an approach no one has ever tried before, well, you might have a genius on your hands.

Right now, too many of these models are black boxes. We don't understand the algorithms. We don't understand how the machines are taught to learn or the information they're being fed relative to the outcomes they get. Sometimes, the outcomes make you scratch your head and say, "Wow, how the hell did that happen?"

Think back to the story I told about Kohler, the faucet maker. It developed a faucet with sensors that turn on when you place your hand under the spigot. However, the faucet consistently failed to work properly for people of color. Now, who the hell was sitting around the table as they dreamed up this concept? Certainly, there were no people of color. No one thought, "Hmm, I wonder what would happen if someone who didn't look like us stuck their hand under here."

Now imagine that a judicial AI, or a sentencing or immigration AI, had the same problem. That would be completely unacceptable. That would defeat the purpose of using AI to diminish the effect of bias. The same issue arises with facial recognition. When facial recognition models think people of color are not humans but animals, we are not going to experience the bias-free convenience we need from technology. I remember meeting a new colleague for the first time at a bank I was hired at. He got my name wrong, using the name of another person of color. When I corrected him, he tried to shrug it off by saying, "Well, you guys look just alike." No, actually we don't. "We do not look anything alike," I told him.

These are the kinds of biases that exist in the physical world that will be transposed to the digital world if we're not careful about who gets seats at the table.

Bias must be at the forefront of our minds as we guide the development of AI. Government can play a huge role in ensuring that these algorithms are accessible and transparent and that we have the opportunity to interrogate them. We must be able to monitor how they are built and trained and have the power to force companies to pivot when outcomes perpetuate what we know to be biased.

In terms of international collaboration, I fear and suspect that the development of AI will mimic the development of vaccines during the pandemic. There will be intense competition to make breakthroughs that singularly benefit one nation. However, we must consider how we can work collaboratively in a way that doesn't leave a significant portion of the world behind. You can easily create two different strata, so how can we work together in a way that doesn't widen that gulf and make that expanse something that can't be navigated or successfully traversed?

The World Is Changing

Imagine a world where no one really works. There is no such thing as a salary. There's no such thing as a job that people do for pay. Most of what happens appears to be automated. What do people do when they don't have to work or many of the things that we work at today are not things we work at tomorrow?

That day may not be terribly far away. How can we ensure people can live comfortably and humanely and pursue a higher level of meaningful work? When we can put robots into hotel rooms to clean them effortlessly and spotlessly, what does it mean for the humans who previously did that work? What does it mean for farmers when robots harvest our crops? What happens to the 100,000 employees of the IRS when AI handles all tax returns, including audits? What happens to cab drivers when self-driving cars take over in our cities? What happens to hundreds of thousands of UPS and Amazon drivers when drones take over home delivery?

San Francisco allows hundreds of autonomous vehicles to traverse the city. There have been accidents and a few men versus machine confrontations. There have been situations where these vehicles have stopped or blocked emergency vehicles. They've caused traffic jams. They've hit people. There are still a number of glitches to work out, but this is the future. San Francisco recognizes that being at the forefront of this is better than being a follower.

It's coming. It's here. I can recall when people initially refused to use ATMs. I remember people wouldn't shop online. Now Amazon is opening stores with no cashiers. You just walk in, show your phone, gather up what you want, and walk out. Your phone is automatically debited. I hesitate to even use this example because, in the time it will take this book to hit the market, these experiences may be so widespread that they may be unsurprising.

I've owned a Tesla since 2017. And while I have not gone all in on full self driving (FSD), other Tesla enthusiasts have. And it's fascinating to watch it. I know my vehicle is tracking and learning from me, even when I'm not using FSD.

And I can't wait for the advent of full self-driving. Today, more than 40,000 people are killed in traffic accidents every year. FSD is not without its problems, but when those are corrected by Tesla or some other auto manufacturers, fatalities and accidents will certainly decline. Again, the federal government needs to be deeply involved in where this is going, ensuring there's an equitable path forward that is inclusive and diverse and delivers outcomes that benefit everyone.

We can't afford to allow factions, however righteous they may be, to drive us to a point of inaction where we sit idly by and let things happen without our involvement. There's a significant danger of that, in terms of how this will unfold and who will benefit or who will bear the burden of unintended consequences.

On the one hand, I'm thrilled about the prospect of advancing technology in our lives. Our lives will be transformed. People will live longer. There's talk that by 2040, we'll be replacing a lot more than just knees and hips, with some sort of technical apparatus. Life could extend to well over

100 years; certainly, your children and grandchildren can expect to live a century or longer.

And that's just life as we know it here on this planet. One of the things I would do as president is issue a John F. Kennedy-like proclamation to establish a permanent station on Mars by the end of the decade. We will go to Mars and back, and we'll have a permanent structure on Mars that houses human life. We are getting close. We are that capable, and I would make that a goal of my administration.

I think it's almost necessary. Given the things we're doing to this planet, I agree with Elon Musk that we need to be thinking about colonizing. If for no other reason than population growth, we need to be thinking about life outside of Earth. Can this planet sustain the number of human beings that we have on it?

It isn't a matter of *if* machines become a staple of our lives. They already are. It's a matter of *how* far this will extend and what will be the benefits and consequences, both planned and unintended.

I was at a conference a couple of years ago where an executive from Google talked about brain augmentation and our kids being a thousand times smarter than we are today because of things we could and would do to manipulate our cerebral capabilities.

That sounds like a "you got to be kidding me" kind of thing, but I have no doubt that will happen. We are going to change ourselves. We are going to augment ourselves. With the total knee replacement I got after my motorcycle accident, I'm already cybernetically enhanced. My knee has a shelf life and will likely need to be replaced at some point. I'm not excited to go under the knife again, but I am excited to see how the replacement knee technology has improved since I got my first replacement. There was a woman at the same conference as the Google executive. Aimee Mullins. She had to have both legs amputated, but that little girl grew up to become a record-setting Paralympics track athlete and a model. She was the first double-amputee to compete in a NCAA Division I track meet. Aimee views her limbs as augmentation she can change. When she wants to be taller, she uses a pair of leg extensions. She also has wooden ones that have ornate carvings that are artistically profound. She views her legs as an enhancement. There's no doubt in my mind that one day, she and others will have an option of putting on human-like legs that have unbelievable capabilities, allowing her to walk faster, run faster, and jump higher—who knows.

There will no doubt be military advancements in augmentation. Russia's Vladimir Putin gave a speech several years ago where he envisioned a future where humans were modified, asserting that it was a threat worse than the atomic bomb. Left unchecked, he said, these enhancements could destroy life as we know it on this planet. No doubt those kinds of things are being contemplated and perhaps worked on in a laboratory somewhere.

The point is that as our government must be consciously, publicly, and transparently in front of this. We must embrace it. We have got to leverage it. We must drive it. We must nurture it. We absolutely need to guide it.

It's almost like a child. We must be actively engaged in how it progresses and is utilized. How do we leverage it and guide it so it has the most positive effect possible on the most people? The alternative is to let it happen and then wrestle with the extraordinary consequences. I prefer the former to the latter.

In either case, I am intrigued. I am cautious, but most of all, I am incredibly excited.

Afterword

Years ago, in a Pittsburgh kindergarten class, a six-year-old looks up to his teacher and answers the perennial question, "What do you want to be when you grow up?" earnestly and confidently:

"I want to be president of the United States."

An answer to cause endearing pride in the child's precocious sense of mission and responsibility, and care for nurturing these qualities. And it would have, were the boy not Black. As it is, the high aspiration becomes disruptive behavior, the idealistic dream a delusional utterance. And instead of loving guidance, the teacher feels compelled to report the worrisome behavior to the boy's mother. It will not be the last time that Ralph Groce will confront a blind obstacle and remain undeterred in his quest for excellence and relevance.

The book you are holding is unusual: It is highly personal, full of stories of lived experiences, but it is not a memoir. It addresses our existential challenges and seeks solutions "to transform this country and the world," but it is not an ideological platform. It is, rather, a heartfelt invitation to a frank conversation about our future, finding our strengths, and coming together to fulfill our promise. Immersed in our daily routines and immediate work, we rarely think at such a high aspirational level and may tend to dismiss or postpone the need to do it. I would like to introduce you to the man behind the message, as I believe his story will help explain the urgency of the conversation.

I met Ralph more than ten years ago at Boston University, where I currently serve as dean of BU's Metropolitan College. He had returned to his alma mater, unsolicited, driven by his belief in the transformative power of education and service. He wanted to understand the areas of greatest need and offer his help—through funding and expert engagement—to meet them. At this time, he had proven himself academically (with two graduate degrees—an MBA and a Master of Urban Affairs) and professionally (with C-level positions at Fortune Global 500 companies and as an entrepreneur and patent holder). Settling in and enjoying the hard-earned comforts of his success was not an option. He was looking for new challenges and ways to give back with the highest impact. Since that first visit, Ralph has been deeply involved in our college and the university—supporting, advising, and motivating us, while also connecting us to other institutions that benefited from his optimistic energy and his gift for problem solving.

Noting the current divisiveness in public discourse across our nation, dwelling on its causes, and bemoaning the insurmountable divide has become a cliché. In my opinion, it is also a dead end. The core principle that Ralph so persuasively presents in this book is unity: build on our strengths to chart a path, find solutions, and join together to implement them. And we have unique strengths in the multiplicity and diversity of opinion and culture, a long tradition of invention unshackled to established thinking, and a relentless can-do spirit. It was a joy reading about these wellsprings of strength and success.

Two themes especially resonated with me. First, the power of entertaining multiple, sometimes contradictory ideas while recognizing the difficulty of bringing them together. Yes, diverse perspectives illuminate different aspects of a problem, but can they be reconciled? Aren't broadly shared beliefs and a uniform culture more conducive to unity? They certainly offer an easier and well-trodden path. Being gracious with those who share one's beliefs and upbringing is pleasant and comfortable. But comfort rarely, if ever, brings novel solutions.

Second, the boldness of grabbing the reader's attention and breaking the conformity of thinking to introduce and explain an important idea: "I never had a job for which I was qualified," states Ralph. Not for lack of education—as noted, Ralph has multiple degrees. And isn't the current mantra "career-ready" education? It is true that people need knowledge and skills to get a job and to keep working longer than at any time in history. At the same time, our global interconnected world, driven by an unprecedented pace of technological change, faces challenges and needs solutions for problems that are unlikely to exist on the syllabus of any course or training program. In addition to a strong academic and professional foundation, tackling these problems hinges on leadership, creativity, and unity of action—building high-performing teams and sustaining a conversation until the job gets done.

These are my personal favorite themes. There are many more worth exploring and thinking about—the impact of AI and technology on society and individual lives, the arts and how they nurture creativity, the critical role of communication, the ability to listen to and hear divergent ideas. I am sure you will find themes meaningful to you within these pages. I hope that you enjoy the lightness and the seriousness of this honest and optimistic book as much as I did.

Tanya Zlateva Ph.D.
Dean, Boston University **Metropolitan College & Extended Education**

www.ingramcontent.com/pod-product-compliance
Lightning Source LLC
Chambersburg PA
CBHW071713020426
42333CB00017B/2246